How to Become Superhuman

"will to power"

Matthew Martin McKissick

Strategic Book Publishing and Rights Co.

Strategic Book Publishing and Rights Co., LLC
USA
www.sbpra.net

For information about special discounts for bulk purchases, please contact Strategic Book Publishing and Rights Co. Special Sales, at bookorder@sbpra.net.

ISBN: 978-1-68235-738-5

Book Design: Suzanne Kelly

Dedication

To all ambitious and driven

Table of Contents

Introduction

The human species has dominated and taken control of the Earth, leaving open ground in which to create their own fate and demise. Through unique genetic makeup and complex of mind, they have shown uncanny abilities to mold or invent new summations. Within the history of tragic events and accomplishments, there have been some who have greatly influenced and stood out from the masses, leading the human race into the new millennium in failure to successes. They are credited with rewriting and changing history with new reforms that gave future generations innovative aspirations to create their own historical imprints.

Within evolutional progression, humans have kept records of every possible exploit affiliated with nature's creation and ideology. While there may be endless material, intellectual explanations in various degrees, as well as systematic dissections of how everything works and purpose, little is known about the humans that have shined in their abilities, allowing them to achieve the impossible, and the motive and drive that led them toward those unimaginable feats. Through influence and achievements, they are forever to be recognized as being something beyond and are perceived as immortal. They are respected and put upon pedestals of greatness to be admired. Because of these rare and fated destinies that were lived in abnormity in sacrifices and enduring challenges, they have contributed to the ever-changing evolution of human existence, giving it profound meaning as each era came and went. While their influence and reason for contribution to advancement may be marveled and appreciated, metaphysically understanding how and what chemical or molecular elements they contained that differed from others that gave them those powers and triggered their inner beings to go forth and achieve the impossible is something no scholar or intellectual has ever figured out or attempted to unveil.

There are endless things that humans have accomplished within physiology, and as modern times have arrived, there came ever-increasing categories in which humans have explored and discovered that their abilities cannot be strictly defined or limited. What has not been done or seen is merely just a short time away from being invented or discovered. But because common society spend most of their lives doing fundamental things like trying to survive, working, and affiliations, they are limited in the amount in which they spend on leisure activities like exploring and inventing, especially if they lack the interest to expand their minds. However if they have the mindset and endeavor to see all the wondrous things that were created, they have the power to obtain it. Through the constant pressures of daily survival, only some have the pleasure of truly fathoming the unimaginable capabilities that have yet to be discovered by basic human structure. Whether singular or mass of populous recognizes the rarity in human physiology to achievements may be irrelevant, because as the human race enters each new era, there continues to be a constant rise in the discoveries of adaptations of all sorts in conditions within perfect genetically made to obscure genetics.

The idea and concept of being superhuman is indefinable, and how one sees and accepts their own accord or variation of being a superior form is a matter of perspective. No person is folly or correct in the assumption of calculative assessment. But within society, there will be and always has been some who have gone beyond the common level of determination to accomplish things that differentiate them as more than just ordinary. The true meaning and representation of a superior being will always be controversial and debated.

At what point should a person be called or accepted as being exceptional? It should not be just one specific area or specialized skill that forms that opinion. Rather, any who shows ability beyond the norm, where their daily lives and rituals are different because of the unorthodox routines that they must follow in order to refine and obtain a higher level of skill and discipline, should be appreciated. While the majority live of intricacies dedicated to a limited time dealing with trials and tribulations, the rare and exceptional have to endure lives where they suppress enjoyment and pleasure. Instead, their daily regimens consist of never-ending struggles and sacrifices of disassociation. Through this discipline and differentiation in rituals and persistence in will to power, they hope to become something of greater worth.

The reason and motive for wanting godly abilities can only be answered by inquisition. If they are not fated by nature and don't feel the inclination within them, then they are not destined or chosen to walk the path of indifference, but for a few, they have to endure certain changes, living isolated lifestyles. Therefore, while the idea of being a superior person may sound great, the consequences and price to be paid in sacrifices of time and the duration of mental focus will be the true test of who is destined to be compared to those who are exempt.

There are three basic elements that comprise human physiology that gives the foundation and separates from other primates, not to diminish or discredit other life-forms don't have the sensitivity. Humans are categorically differentiated in intellect compared to every other species. Through their ability to rationalize, humans have distinguished themselves as being in a different realm of importance. Whether or not there ever can be a better way to express the grounds and merits in understanding the complexity and rarity of flesh beings, within the predestined order to be followed, humans have founded and been induced into ideals and ideologies in which to express themselves and to revolutionize.

Within the three components of physiology—mind, body, and soul—humans have explored and challenged themselves in their ability to reach and go beyond what is expected for the purpose of seeking and finding the truth behind the mysteries of the unforeseen to the possible toward the unattainable. Therefore, through earliest advancements of human physiology and whatever era of accomplishments, humans continue to explore and challenge themselves, showing endless capabilities and avenues to endure and overcome. The reason and purpose of circumventing into such depth and breaking the barriers of normality is controlled by the force of nature, within populous, there's always going to be those who are destined to be something of a phenomena amongst the masses. They will become an imprint that society will either admire or desecrate.

Whether they find to be blessed or cursed in whatever suffering or praise they may receive or endure will all be irrelevant and incomprehensible to others, because as new ideas come and go in productive to destructive, the motion of life will continue to flow without any remorse within struggles and pain of desired. Because within the masses of the imperfect and emotionally compromised, there always will be opinions within acceptance to rebuke. Whatever accomplishment or failure that has been set forth and proclaimed to be in precedence of superiority. They will be insignificant or meaningless, as each naive mind perceives and understands the true meaning of being superhuman differently.

Mind

The first thing to be considered is the mind. Although it's the main motor that is essential and to which other elements are connected in function and the awareness of consciousness, the mind has its own depth of challenges and barriers to be crossed in reaching for superior ability. Through the power source of the mind, humans have both achieved and failed in attempts to discover and reach for things beyond. They may also have cursed themselves in wanting to enter into the abyss of godly secrets, where some have even gone beyond the reasoning of logic in which to obtain the knowledge of superiority. Humans were fated and predestined to explore and discover things unknown, to give them some kind of solace and reasoning in existence. Through their inquisitive appetites of needing to evolve and progress, certain individuals have designated themselves to go about discovering, proclaiming ownership, and finding recognition.

The mind is representative of the brain and is one whole organ that has a few compartments, but the complexity of the design and function is incomprehensible. Hence, while other forms of life, whether on land or in the ocean, have some kind of brain in which to drive them to construct with common components, somehow their function is a lesser degree of complexity to understanding the cause and effects. This is true even in the closest relation to humans, chimpanzees, whose genetic sequence is merely a fraction different. But within their distinct and designated placement of origin in evolution, they are nowhere near as complex in social development and intellectual capabilities. Therefore, although all living species have similar brain components, structure, and function, in the inner workings and its ability to go beyond in creativity and calculative assessments, no other living thing can compare.

Since the earliest humans comprehensively reached for inner sanctums of discovering and understanding themselves, the journey of wondering began, and through progressive changes, there came avenues in which humans could calculate and research previous ancestors' existences and their own future. Within decades of discovering ancient relics or various documents and doctrines of the past, scholars have explored and made calculative assessments of how humans existed from the earliest. Through these innovative skills and awareness toward existence and desiring a greater understanding of themselves, the human mind has been fated and predestined to enter the world of the unknown, and they will be cursed to become their own crucifixion.

Humans were destined to change and revolutionize, and certain individuals were fated to become examples of endless possibilities that they could accomplish or be persecuted in attempts to discover the knowledge of the unknown. Through curiosity and the ambition of wanting to understand and achieve personal intuitions, they endured the mental faculties and challenges. The depth and style of the painstaking deprivation of mental strain came in various forms, but the particular situations in endearment may have been within the control of an ancestor's bloodline, being an obsolete choice in nature's coercion to displacement. For example, although humans have thought and envisioned goals of desire and need, through nature's assistance in displacing circumstances and situations, individuals were forced to take unorthodox paths to reach toward intended mission. Although they have calculatedly processed their thoughts systematically to follow certain logical steps in hope of finding the pathway to correct answers, because the human mind is always imperfect in its flesh, the force of nature coerced or manipulated the direction that must be taken in order to achieve success.

The unexpected predicament of conflict may exist in many different times. Hence, individuals that were on a mission to discover new and innovative things often felt condemned and forsaken. And because the length of time it took to accomplish their goal, with all sorts of uncertainty, confusion, mental turmoil, and unimaginable circumstances to overcome in breaking barriers to a higher level of understanding, individuals were left alone in a darkened and isolated world, where they slowly began to lose the reason of logic and ever so slowly became diluted. In turn, their inner being became hardened, leading to a path of self-destruction. While a few have overcome, there were others who couldn't handle the strain of mental deprivation and chose to eliminate themselves from the competitiveness of will to power.

Although the mind is merely an invisible particle of energy that's deeply secreted in the brain, within human ideas and creativity, there is an array of areas in which the mind is responsible in its depth of achieving greatness toward superhuman feats or accomplishments. Through human standards and an acclaimed system of relevance, they have put certain achievements and creativity within the realm of superiority. Even though humans have categorically created a systematical order of higher to lower significance, to any other life-form existing even on the outer limits of Earth, human inventions and ideas have no meaning or value. Therefore, although humans may pride themselves in accomplishments to whatever depth, it's merely an illusion that they believe has some significance.

Nevertheless, as humans advance through whatever period of time, they are forever destined to revolutionize into a more perfected species. In turn, within never-ending challenges and struggles with endless sacrifices and casualties, they must continuously pursue to become superior, to prove themselves, whether for personal gratification, finding an easier livelihood, or fame and recognition. Whether the motive for an individual's pursuit of mental challenges is valid or irrelevant, everything in existence, from the natural order to the dispositions of species, are all predestined to be in achieved or failed, and it'll all be recorded and become added to the documents of history, which will give greater visions for the next generations to follow or disregard.

The mental strain or suppression of the mind has been there from the beginning of time. It is an element that must exist with evolutional change. Without it, nothing can evolve; everything would stay in the same simplistic state. Therefore, with the passage of time in the human race, certain individuals were destined to become the building blocks that gave a stronger sense of value to finding better calculative assessments in understanding the power of the mind. Mental turmoil and suppressions were often made by an individual's obsessive madness, which in turn put them in harsh or inhumane situations, likes various artists and intellectuals who tried to break through the barriers of normality. Others found themselves in unfortunate circumstances of manmade conflicts like war, various isolated institutions such as prisons, or all kinds of mental instabilities after succumbing to substance abuse. Whether the individuals were naturedly coerced to endure mental strain from natural disasters or misfortunes, or it was their own doing, they all had to endure and overcome extreme mental depravities that words cannot simply justify or give solace in times of endearment. Because no beings are ever given a choice in existence, whatever predicaments they have inflicted upon makes them merely innocent victims of nature's cruelty.

However, on the basis of give and take in all the unimaginable and incomprehensible things in creation, there must be some consequences for all the beauty and wondrous things that existence contains. Just as matter must contain two different particles, negative and positive, humans are fated to face and endure certain forms of pain and suffering. The energy of life and existence are in constant motion and create continual friction that cannot be seen by sight. Although humans may see and accept the fundamental concept of how energy moves both inside and outside of objects, it's hard to objectively understand and perceive the flesh of beings as energy, unlike other things that are presumed less complex. Because the energy must be in constant motion and be dispersed into something through the inevitable necessity and needed combustion in which to maintain life and universe cohesively, humans must continuously evolve, because the outer appearance of flesh and bones are nothing more than just coated elements of invisible particles. Any time the energy travels and speeds up, it increases the frequencies and platform of its original state. Hence, when humans try to explore and obtain deeper understanding, it changes the rotation of intervals from normal society, but the consequences and effects in which an individual must experience to endure is something that can only be adhered by their own summations in reason and purpose of omission.

While materials change in energy, the consequences of which, good to bad, will be of benefit, in the human condition, the alteration of energy could be costly to an individual's life. All things are made of energy, and humans are no different, existing through particles of energy, not what they were condition to believe, likes the reproductive system or hormones. Through the manmade and imperfect species of being, humans have a systematical way of controlling the flow of society and race. Whether in the earliest times or whatever era, they are and always will be conditioned, in certain reforms of breeding, to socially adapt themselves to particular beliefs and meaning of life. Because of that, they automatically have a transfixed mental particle of energy in a certain specified frequency, in which they are trained and disciplined from conception to whatever time they live, from infancy to development to death.

When a living being has formed and entered the physical world of life, it must move and produce a certain trait of motion. While all the other natural living beings have their own distinct pattern of movements, humans, within complex social systems of behaviors and diverse characteristics, have more profound effects and reasons. Therefore, no matter what period or time, when a human infant is born, they must endure the same fundamental mental strain or suppression of isolation in which to prepare themselves for future cultural affiliation. Although babies do not recognize the struggles and mental obstacles that they must overcome, such as walking, adapting to their new surroundings, or becoming a fully adjusted person, as they reach a certain phase of adolescence, they will feel the strain of mental anguish and frustration being a human includes, like academic tests to a personal need for accomplishment. As they pass through academic years and achieve their parent's intended goal of graduation, they will continue the mental suppression by having to obtain an occupation in which to support themselves.

Commonly, humans will not recognize that they are being suppressed, because their minds are distracted by different waves of frequency intertwined with pleasurable emotions in association of life. And the moments of mental suppressions are limited to certain times and situations, rather than having to suffer continuously for years or decades. Only then will they recognize the negative aspects of existence and become vulnerable to self-destruction. However, usually if an individual only goes through a spurt of an experience on the downside of life, eventually they'll bounce back with some kind of positive reason for living, such as having a good job, personal hobbies, relationships, or being able to obtain some gratification from materialistic things. Through the humanistic appetite of the needs of the flesh, humans can easily be persuaded to see the brighter side of life, especially with support from loved ones, modern medication, and even through the affection of other organisms. In turn, they'll block the darkness out and superficially believe that they are free and never see themselves as a prisoner of existence. Nevertheless, no matter what the age, all humans must endure a certain amount of time in isolation, boredom, and most importantly the mental strain of being of flesh.

It's these unfortunate, unwelcome words of metaphysical obstacles and challenges that are the best contributors and pathways to human's greatest periods of discoveries and inventive ideas. Unfortunately, however, whatever the true meaning and purpose of reforming the human breed to certain specifications is, it may be irrelevant because within the massiveness of the population, there always will be success and failure, and having an unaccountable succumbing toward negativity in an unfulfilled agenda to will not stop the continual functioning of society. The automated conditions of human life in having a home, a family, and superficial attachments have created a mental psychosis that must be maintained and for generations to come. Anything foreign that alters will be considered abnormal or alien within the tradition of a specific race. Through these transfixed beliefs and social structure, humans have developed a platform for future members of society to follow, but through constant evolutional change and improvising themselves to be better, they are cursed and fated to cross the barriers of structure, and certain individuals will be chosen to be an example, a sacrifice, for the ambition of wanting a superior form.

To have a basic understanding of the concept of the frequency change of energy in wanting to penetrate deeper in the progression of speed is simple. To break the barrier of normality, there must be some kind of force that increases the acceleration. When an individual is trying to obtain the power of beyond and it triggers the subconscious mind in attempt to find the secrets of godly powers, it has disturbed the frequency of the conditioned mind. As it goes deeper into the subconscious and the uncertainty of thoughts, the mind must journey and endure some uncomfortable and unpredictable things while breaking through the barriers. Although common people don't understand the geometrics of how an individual can obtain a higher level of energy in the mind, if they were to observe all the individuals that have higher mind power and skills, they would understand that all they need is some kind of silent mental meditation, which is usually known in the spiritual realm.

There are all sorts of examples of how the power of the mind is increased by focused discipline, and no matter what kind of mental energy an individual obtains—academics, physical, or spiritual—they all contain the same fundamental element of persistent quietness for an amount of time. The increase of energy can only be obtained through steady progression, no matter the particular area, and depending on the degree and level of power it wants to achieve, the amount of time and persistence also differs. The greater the power and higher level of energy an individual wants to obtain, the increase in the number of sacrifices they must give and endure toward mental suppressions. Therefore, in order to achieve the highest level of mental ability, it has little to do with academic intellect. It is rather how long an individual can withstand the silence of isolation and determination to adapt to different and uncomfortable situations and experiences.

Humans are forced to fit into the mold of society, and they must follow certain rules and regulations of their distinctive race. Whether an individual believes in the same ideology or not is irrelevant, because within the constant needs for the necessities in which to survive, every individual experiences some amount of isolation or suffers from the deprivation of freedom. Hence, no one is totally free. All humans spend a certain amount of time in a form of incarceration. While society may naively define very flat guidelines of who's free or not—like prisoners because they can't come and go as they please—within daily life, whether its worrying about survival or dealing with personal addictions, every individual, children and adults, must be suppressed and imprisoned in some form for a certain amount of time, even though they don't perceive it that way because they justify it as being a ritual part of life in a society. When a child is at the proper age, they must enter an institution of learning, and that will continue until they graduate. Soon after that, they must enter another kind of institution to begin some kind of job. Although the individuals don't see themselves as confined but rather earning a living, because of the pressure of survival and supporting loved ones, they are confined in working environment. They cannot leave and must abide by the rules of a particular job position that they may like or dislike until they have put in a certain amount of time as penance.

Even though the non-criminals in a society feel that they are free and everything they do is of their own accord—i.e., have the freedom to roam and do as they please—if they think again, could they really leave current circumstances without worries or concerns about future well-being? In prison, where all the individuals have acted out in selfishness and caused some harm to society, and whom the society believes are being punished, have nothing to worry about as far as paying bills, keeping a job, or the daily pressure of knowing where they will be and sleep. Nevertheless, no matter how an individual perceives and understands life—for instance, knowing certain people have better lifestyles than others—everyone from the righteous to the sinners will serve a certain amount of time in isolation, deprived from the pleasures of life.

In those moments of confinement and depravity, the human mind has the best pathway to creativity, breaking through the barriers of godly wisdom to the unattainable. It's all about sharpening the individual's mental focus and improving themselves so that the mind is challenged to its maximum. If a person never suffers hunger and has everything easily accessible, they will never break through normality and become as stagnate as motionless objects. Although societies have never-ending social conflicts and differences in life dispositions, like being rich or poor, its individuals who lives in hardship that have the best chances of reinventing themselves and discovering superior abilities. Nevertheless, through the desire and motive to be better and more productive, humans have no other alternative but to continue to abide by the rules of society, no matter the degree of mental stress or conflicts. In turn, they have imprisoned themselves without ever knowing that they've been persecuted without a trial and given up freedom of choice.

While certain degrees of mental strain are adaptable, such as contributing to society by working, there are other situations that are not as easily accepted and are more severe. Some of these are through personal accord, like various pioneers seeking new ideas and discoveries or entrepreneurs and creative intellectuals, while others are due to natures cruelty, the injustice of natural disasters and enduring aftereffects. For the former, through their naivety and ambition-driven appetites, they assumed to know everything and risked everything, from finances to personal well-being, toward future success. They were trying to break new ground and invested daily existence in the search for something that wasn't practical in society's eyes and which they knew might be something illogical. However, in their desire to succeed, they put themselves in harsh and difficult mental situations.

The problem with finding innovative ideas, in both the practical business sense and the visual perception, is that it requires a stillness of mind. An individual must be in tune with nature's energy, where there must be no other sounds or distractions to disrupt the energy of focus from accelerating to new heights, although mechanical objects merely need adjustments to achieve an increase in power, but for internal working of the mind, the best and most effective method to increase power is continual frequency of energy found in long silences. Within that silence, the mind is able to accelerate and become acute and more observant toward its intended goal. While machinery basically just needs human ingenuity to achieve its intended power, for human's internal membrane, it takes a little more than just few screws or additional parts.

The method and style of increasing human power versus machines is a totally different spectrum of understanding. From birth, humans are conditioned in an environment surrounded with various sounds and abstracted things. Within this colorful upbringing, the mind adapts and continues to proceed in the same fundamental process as the infant grows and develops. While other life-forms grow simply—to eat or get eaten until death—humans are far more complex in growth and development, where their perception and internal way of thinking changes depending on social surroundings. However, no matter what social structure a human infant is born into, privileged or not, they all have the same fundamental upbringing with family and friends. In turn, their minds adapt to certain conditioned frequency waves, where the energy is constantly eradicated through daily mannerisms and efforts at survival. Hence, they do a lot of things that require only a fraction of mental focus, from domestic things and relationships to the intellectual pursuits.

The only time the human mind requires additional sources of energy is when they enter certain occupations, and while they may use more mental power and focus, with experience and time they'll adapt, and the job becomes as easy as changing clothes or brushing teeth. In turn, the mind no longer needs to focus; it's almost as if they can do tasks blindfolded. Therefore, while at first the mind has to increase in power to understand specialized tasks or skills, through years and decades of the same repetitive motion, the mind relaxes and its frequency is sustained according to need. So, through reformed patterns of function, human minds have adapted to certain conditions, and that will not change in acceleration until the individual changes the dynamic in lifestyle. Therefore, when an individual wants to break free from normal mind function and is seeking to find a new creative discovery or innovative idea, they will have to change society's conditioned lifestyle and experience another dimensional world full of possibilities.

When an individual journeys into the abyss for an opportunity to seek the unknown power of superiority, they must forgo their fundamental lifestyle and live in solitude, where the mind can think clearly and be observant of its surroundings. Hence, the emotional bonds of family and friends must be sacrificed to allow the mind to receive the sensitive flow of energy in which to obtain the secrets that are hidden within the subconscious. Not only that, they must aggressively explore the different intricacies in jobs and social situations. While they may naively feel the euphoric highs of enthusiasm at the beginning, as time passes without achieving any success or compensation for all the effort that has been put forth, the mental strain will begin to wear them down, possibly leading to depression or self-destructive behavior.

The problem of not fulfilling an individual's ideas is not the major complication. Rather, individuals must find ways in which to maintain and establish a refuge for refueling the body. While the earliest part of journey was blissful, filled with high hopes despite even a lack of financial resources, as time passes in their seclusion with a lack of positive results and having nothing to fall back on, most importantly always being financially strapped, and individual will be confronted within two choices—either find a way to continue or give up. If an individual has family and friends to help them, they may be in better position, but it'll also be their weakest link, destroying the prospects of breaking through the barriers of the unknown and continuously expanding their mind. In wanting to obtain superior knowledge and find new innovative and creative ideas, the indefinite price and consequences of depravity in survival is the essential element that will teach the best of lessons in understanding the world. If they have friends and family helping with financial and emotional support, not only will it prolong the journey, but the individual has not put forth the true dedication that a lack of resources demands. Nevertheless, if individual is destined to succeed, whether among friends or associates, they will still always be alone whilst thinking about personal ambitions.

Unfortunately, as years of surviving with the constant twists and turns of dealing with limited resources and being mentally and physically drained, the original optimistic outlook slowly darkened. The problem of time passing without successful results is not the killer of desire. Rather, it is the constant pressure of fulfilling basic human needs that will finally end the journey. All extremists or those obsessed have one-track minds; they feel they must spend all their time and energy toward interests. They tend to neglect or avoid other necessities, like trying other things to gain a greater perspective. Instead, they seclude themselves. This phenomenon will cause the most amount of mental strain, causing individuals to go insane when nature intervenes by diverting their attention from singular thought process. Things will either end in chaos or they will have to start all over again.

Although there may be all sorts of available jobs, through an individual's prejudice to social adaptation, they have preferences in occupational choice, from the highest paying to the most beneficial. While at first the individual will take and do any kind of job, the never-ending struggle with finances or poor working conditions will eventually lead them to do outlandish things that will cause complications. Even if an individual finds and obtains a comfortable job, their personal lifestyle will eventually wear that down, and they will enter into the world of poverty, but that is a crucial in helping break through the barrier of the undiscovered. It's during the years of deprivation and the uncertain pathway to success that an individual will make their ultimate decision of continuing on or eliminating themselves from the world of competition. Besides not having the continuous flow of financial resource to support themselves, the seeker or opportunist also must be content with the mental conditions, from anguish to the voices of insanity, where the conscious and subconscious are in a constant bipolar battle. Because the individual has been dissociative single-minded on the mission, they neglect basic human needs like socialization or maintaining physical appearance. Through the years of isolation, they become darkened and lost souls, a contrast from the beginning when they were energetic and full of life. They seem to have aged, are less energetic about life, and have no interest in the things in which they were conditioned from childhood. In their attempt to discover the mystery and secrets of superior ability, they've cocooned themselves in a mental shell, and they are just short way from being swallowed by an imaginary world of indifference. But if they survive and overcome the demons of insanity, they will eventually prevail and find some kind of solace in fulfilling their vision.

While the success or failure of mental deprivation in chasing personal dreams and ambitions lies in perspective, there are other situations in which humans have to endure an indefinite amount of mental challenges that society often neglects to give credence to, where the mind is tormented with such extreme levels of darkness that they can't function normally and go mad. While some have survived the ordeal, others chose to ease their suffering within the confines of various mental institutions or, in extreme cases, entering the unknown world of peace and tranquility in death. In the trials and tribulations of unexpected social conflicts and indifferences, they have succumbed or been subjected to misfortunes. In turn, they become victims of unfortunate circumstances that challenge their mental faculties to the extreme. This can include things like social tragedies, war, natural disasters, and even diseases.

In any event, whether the tragedy was caused by the individual or through human error or corruption, they all had to endure unimaginable degrees of mental anguish. But through will to survive, for whatever reason, they were willing to accept and adapt to those circumstances in the hope of being free from the bondage of darkness.

Some examples are individuals who were trapped in a foreign environment or culture, where they endured endless mental or physical pain for years without comfort of any kind. Because of unexpected events, the individuals had to survive in impossible odds, where their very existence was in danger of being extinguished. Not getting proper daily nutrition or knowing their whereabouts was bad, but being able to slow the mental breakdown and maintaining the will to survive was more mentally challenging than outsiders could ever imagined. While many have not made through such a fateful experience, there were a few who somehow defied the odds in will to survive, making experts wonder and marvel at the capacity and level of human mental abilities.

In other situations, such as individuals being taken as hostages for unforeseen reasons, or kids and adults being used in human trafficking, those people were promised certain compensation for business ventures or other opportunities but instead were caged like animals and fed a minimal amount of food and had limited sanitation. Besides not being treated humanely and having their freedom taken away, they were denied any other human contact. While some survived and regained freedom, their mental stability and perception of life changed so drastically that they no longer felt and functioned as normal. They were so trapped in mental turmoil that they feared returning to society, continuing to hide in darkness, isolated with all kinds of mental dementia. Then there are others who had to endure the most extreme suffering and human indignation, like prisoners of war or even death-row inmates. Although some punishment may be looked on as deserving in the case of criminals, understanding the mental turmoil and anguish they have to endure and the strength of mind to overcome and survive is something that outsiders can never imagine.

While all individuals who had to endure mental cruelty and suffering must be appreciated for the amount of discipline and focus it takes to survive and overcome, it is hard to compare that to what prisoners of war had to endure in the old days in distant jungles or the interrogation of political prisoners being held in inhumane conditions. Any kind of modern imprisonment is almost comfortable and pleasurable compared to that. Being punished for individual crimes or enduring consequences for opposition in war may justify the particular situations to be endured, but on the basis that all minds have the same fundamental strains of pain and anguish, it's hard for society to fathom the degree of depression an incarcerated person or war victim endured, especially with the monotonous, repetitive rituals and suffocation of those sentenced to decades or even life in prison. While outsiders may spend their days doing various activities, a prisoner's day is spent with minimal things in which to occupy the mind, which causes them to enter a world of darkness, where time seems to stop without hope for the future. In these situations of confinement, restriction of freedom, and living in small spaces in uncivilized conditions, individuals must somehow find a sense of self-worth in which to overcome the displacement of isolation. The range and degree of mental suffering cannot be truly defined with words. When it comes to casualties of war or victims that succumbed to disease before modern medicine, especially in tyrannic socialist systems, the level of mental anguish and suffering cannot be expressed in a way where an outsider could ever feel or understand the breaking point that must be conquered in those extreme conditions.

In life, all beings have to endure a certain degree of deprivation and suffering; unfortunately, the more the pain, the better it is to break through the barrier of naivety and obtain the wisdom of the beyond. Although these experiences may darken the emotions within individuals and affect their well-being and future success, all life-forms must endure a cèrtain level of abandonment and isolation at some point, which will make them stronger and give them more perspective. In those moments, the mind has the greatest potential for growth, development, and focus in purpose. And even though most members of society never see themselves as suppressed or isolated because they are fulfilling basic human needs or raising a family, whenever they are detached from that environment, whether it's because of work obligations or the inevitable experiences in developing process, it's something that must be considered.

It starts out early in life, when every child must learn to leave their comfortable environment of a parent's home and enter into the unknown world of social adaptation and intellectual development in preschool. While at beginning the child will cry because of its new challenges and obstacles, it must be experienced and will be a great influence in helping them grow, develop, and have a stronger sense of individuality. Hence, children are isolated and suppressed all through their developing years. And when entering into work force, they continue the suppressive journey as long as they continue to exist in the constant demand to maintain a certain standard of living. While these kinds of confinement in a suppressive life may seem the choice of the individuals, realistically, to survive and meet daily need, every individual that wants to live must be suppressed and overcome it by whatever means. Otherwise, they'll have limitations and become lost and have to depend on others for survival. So, whether an individual is coerced by nature or they've put themselves in certain suppressive situations, it's the inevitable dues all living beings must pay to exist. Through the life force of energy in the embodiment of love and the naive belief in important values, humans have justified their existence not as a curse, but instead accepted the consequences and recognized life as a blessing.

Body

The human body is mostly comprised of cells and liquid, which are fused by molecules of different elements, and it is vulnerable to foreign invaders both internally and externally. Although humans have shown great physical ability in capacity for survival and showmanship, compared to the genetic makeup of other species, human physiology isn't as durable. Rather, they are more susceptible to being tarnished and deteriorate easily. Because the human body is simply made and consists of tissues, bones, and water, it can easily be damaged or harmed by simple things likes of paper cuts, household chemicals, bacterial irritation of the skin, and infectious diseases. While other species may have their own genetic defects, nothing is as imperfect and perfect at the same time as human physiology. They can transform their natural state into armor that provides defensive protection and assists in offensive attacks in battles. Through the conditioning and altering of internal and external layers of skin and molecules, the human body can achieve unconventional superior abilities that others could never perceived. While other organisms made evolutional change in physicality with minimal effect, humans have overcome their deficiency of being the weaker primate and have dominated in making themselves physically superior.

The metamorphosis of the human body came slowly and was unnoticeable for long period of time, but the physiology began progressively changing from the earliest. It's just that the degree and depth in which the transformation took form were hardly recognized as important or necessary. However, through the inevitable advancement that put humans on the pathway to becoming superior, they've also been changing metaphysically, upgrading and improving conditions that give them better awareness and survival sense. While it may be debatable whether the first very human form was strong or weak, as evolution and nature's influences took hold, humans metamorphosized into something better and stronger.

Although humans have endured and taken painful steps in their struggles to advance, because they could not control the surroundings they lived in, they were merely going through the motions that had been planted by an unknown force that guided them toward the unattainable. In turn, through intuition and the desire to overcome deficiencies, they have followed internal instincts to become greater than they were. Through this metamorphic analogy of how humans made progressive pathways through trials and tribulation, they were nothing more than puppets that were coerced to do what was destined to be. But the price and the consequences suffered in triumphs to defeats had individuals internally questioning the reason for the journey.

Even though humans were initially the weakest physically and were vulnerable to potentially destructive foreign invaders, they were destined to become the dominant ruler of all other forms. They were able to transform and obtain the knowledge and skills that gave them their rightful place. Through the experiences and unorthodox ways of nature's intrusion in the form of obstacles and challenges, lessons to be learned toward greater sensibilities, individuals had to experience and endure unpleasant situations in personal anguish or life-threatening events, such as the cause and effect of social conflicts, war, natural disasters, famine, and economic recessions. Since humans themselves do not have the wisdom of how to perfect the imperfect, making them better specimens, it is natural forces that coerce the human race to endure, overcome, and obtain skills they lack. And while there were many circumstances where those experimenting couldn't endure the journey and ended in tragedies, there were others who overcame adversities and became examples of how an imperfect species can obtain the unthinkable or impossible, no matter what kind of situation they faced.

While articulate words may define and explain the reason and purpose for an individual's misfortunes in life, the motionless time of days or years they had to endure can never be sanctified by mere literary prose. In earliest existence, it can be assumed that the human body wasn't as challenged as it is in modern times because of the volume of resources and limited population. However, as Earth filled with more occupants and resources declined, unforeseen crises affected the mechanics of survival, causing the body to adapt to unexpected abnormalities, such as withstanding the stagnation of daily regimens, mental strain caused by economic recessions and natural disasters, and malnutrition to the point that the body had to handle extreme physical fatigue. Sometimes it was simply lacking food or having to endure a lack of water when traveling long distances during migrations, forcing the body to overcome muscle tiredness and exhaustion.

As advancement took hold and humans entered the modern world, the depth and diversity of man created a whole new interpretation of what was impossible in achieving superhuman feats that could only have been envisioned in fantasy. As the old and simplistic human endeavors were revolutionized into new reforms, the depth to which humans would endure pain, suffering, and sacrifices would be recognized and justified in their desire to be of greater worth, which has changed the pages of the past and recorded a new perspective in ideologies, reinventing themselves into something greater than they could have ever fathomed. But the disciplines that were expected will only be foreshadowed by the desire to overcome adversary of limitations.

It all started out with innocent children acting out an imaginary world of adventure and excitement, but through the curse of fate to the inevitable evolutional change of progression, the childlike playfulness turned more intense as the human race advanced and created avenues in which characters made through fantasy came alive. But the consequences for creating or reinventing a new species with the superior ability to survive and adapt were more than what the innocence of children wished for or would like to have experienced. Although the childlike visions and scenarios of battles against the evil and powers to be obtained were illusions of the mind, to have them actually transform into reality was more than they could have ever envisioned.

The first stepping stone humans had to endure was simply taking the motherly nourished body into a new form by conditioning and harnessing it, like melting mineral ores and refining them into more specified means, developing them into denser materials. Even though the human diet changed into more solid foods with all kinds of nutrients, it still has limitations in vitality and performance compared to other primates. Almost all newborn infants in every species are fed and nourished from their mother's womb, which contains a milky substance full of nutrients. Although this is the natural and automated system of nourishing for strong and healthy beings, the human makeup of flesh and its chemical components are different. Hence, while the milky substance may look the same in texture and color, the potency and effects to bone and tissue are different. Because of these differences, the wild species are stronger in all aspects of physiological survival, including vulnerability to disease. Nevertheless, within the transformation of the evolutional progression, humans were fated to change the vulnerable state of simplicity and weaknesses by trying to duplicate the skills and abilities of their primitive companions, trying to perfect the imperfections and condition themselves into something beyond natural state.

As humans strived to be stronger and obtain better conditions in which to adapt and progress into a better species of beings, they put themselves in predicaments and challenges like the world of competition in sports and athletics. While the exact pretense and motives for creating different sport competitions can always be argued, the advancement and endurance of physical challenges began even before mankind gave recognition. Through the importance of evolutional growth and advancing in adaptation, humans have created an array of activities and specialized events in which to prove their superiority and self-worth. And through these manmade festivals of competitiveness, certain individuals took their bodies to extreme levels in performance, enduring unlimited degrees of physical challenges and tiredness.

Even though physicality began before they were consciously aware of it, what humans have done from the earliest days to modern times is nothing new. Rather, it's the old ways of ancestry's automated cycle of life, especially those found in ancient written documents and biblical stories. As humans evolved and modernized themselves, improving their ability to survive, the mechanics and fundamental necessities of tools and their physiological makeup did not change. Instead, it has intensified and been reinvented into a more civilized way as humans continually strive to be a better and more perfect breed. Therefore, as human race proceeds and continues into whatever millennium, they are to forever endure and achieve superhuman things.

There are all sorts of activities that challenge the human physiology both externally and internally. While in primitive time it may simply have been to obtain skills in hunting to producing great amounts of energy to survive, but as time passed and revolutionized, the gimmicks and methods of conditioning and showing specialized skills became more commercial and personalized ambitions, rather than being just a need for survival. Nevertheless, whether humans attain superior physical attributes for personal gain or out of necessity, all who consciously attempt it or are coerced by nature by unexpected tragedies must exhibit the same type of physical duration in discipline and struggles.

Words can easily express and explain the stepping stone of what is expected and needed in the journeys to overcome and achieve, but the depth of pain and physical anguish in the years or decades of endearment can never be justified by outsider's admiration and retrospect of understanding the individuals in turmoil. Nevertheless, the journeys of defying and conquering the unimaginable, impossible feats of achievement will never end. Instead, there will be other new ideals that will destroy and upgrade human physiology toward greater heights, elevating the most dominant species of being into new forms that will give future generations something to admire and give possible avenues in overcoming their worst adversary of self-doubt and believing themselves to be of greater worth.

The modern era has induced and subjected the human body to be used and abused in such extreme transformations that at times it's hard to believe it's simply made of cells and liquid. And while there are extremes of how far a body's physiology can metamorphosize, various athletes have transformed physicality into new heights in the most unorthodox ways, bloating or condensing themselves from one extreme to another, from oversized obesity to the slimness of distance runners. On one hand, the flesh is stretched so far from its original form that it endangers all the internal organs from being crushed from pressure of overexertion, to the point that it's hard to believe the individual is still able to breath and live normally. On the other hand, like that of Olympic marathon runners, the skin and cells are so drained and condensed that the body is endanger of using muscle tissues and other internal organs for needed fuel, taking the body beyond the standard and pressuring it toward failure, to the point of being out of fuel and passing out from fatigue and lack of nutrients. Somehow, through the discipline of years of training and adaptation, the body is able to adjust in accordance with the necessities of the immune system and somehow achieve the impossible. Then there are other examples likes of bodybuilders who have hardened their liquid molecules into something so hard that it tightens the cell tissues so that they become very dense, almost as strong as concrete or steel.

While harnessed and sculpted images of flesh may be easily appreciated, the decades of training and discipline it took to obtain it can only be understood by the individual fulfilling a desire to do so. No matter what ways human flesh has been trained and conditioned to adapt to become something superior, human physiology has shown there are no limits to its capabilities, that it can achieve the impossible, even to extreme and dangerous situation of hiding objects internally. Through the obsessive or necessity of survival, human body has shown various depth to methods in which the flesh of simplicity can be altered to certain specification in development of perfection or distortion. The reason why an individual feels the need to change their natural state into another is part of the distinct natural order, like they are merely following the internal instructions of what nature has intended for them in particular life journey.

Whether the individuals are in control of their transformation or being coerced by nature's unexpected misfortunes, some had to endure and overcome unexpected experiences and deformities, such as people who got lost and were abandoned in some desolate place without resources for survival, or an individual who wanted to induce their body to reach beyond the superficial world and its commercialized influences of body deformations, even within spiritual practices of hunger deprivation and fasting. The human body has been challenged in many ways, showing how the flesh can be altered in success to failure—for instance, in the extreme and dangerous situations where the internal cavities of the body were used for storage for transporting valuable objects for capital gains, or concealing weapons that can easily rupture and cut the organs, like convicts or those criminally-minded.

Just as the achievements and journey individuals endure and their feelings of accomplishment or failure will never be known except by them, the time, pain, and agony that they had to suffer in can also can only be justified by them alone. Because there are so many degrees and variations in which the human body has been conditioned and metamorphosized to distortion, it's hard to detect and explain every possible way the flesh has been challenged. Therefore, while there may be endless ways in which the flesh has been corrupted and condition to perform superior feats, there are other extreme transformations that must be paid some kind of tribute in understanding and appreciation, because the degree and depth of complication and danger in achieving them is beyond reasoning. Whether they are recognized as sensible or illogical freaks because of being extreme, like all kinds within the superficial world of physical distortions in sumo wrestling or even common people who are extremely overweight, these individual exists in every category and circumstance in which the human body has been subjected to impossible odds. While there are more failures than successes, the time of dedication and endearing the painstaking persistence is something that can never be expressed by words.

While the visual images and recorded documents of the impossible being conquered, like Greek mythology and biblical stories, may easily be appreciated, to become something unrealistic from a fantasy world of dreamers, there's an underlining that must be adhered to and recognized. The problem of representing the image of a superior being is that it takes time and persistence, with endless personal sacrifices to society's standard beliefs and ideologies. And while fighting and believing in an individual's cause and reason for a particular journey in life may be hard enough, to become something abnormal takes more time, dedication, and effort than many want to accept. Hence, while countless want to be, only a few will ever surpass the journey of becoming. Therefore, while there are, and will always be, endless numbers who attempt to be and do so with just a few years of dedication, there's a fine line as to what degree the individual has broken the barrier of normality. There's a great distance between the short-lived and maintaining prolonged decades of doing the same repetitive things and continuously sacrificing personal needs and social affiliations.

Every individual has the potential to become whatever superior form they desire, no matter how imperfectly they may see their genetic makeup. All individuals have the ability to become anything they desire, if they feel the inclination, but it is easier said than done. When an individual is shown some kind of recognition after overcoming impossible odds, the image of the pain and suffering that comes with accomplishment are never seen or felt by onlookers; they only see the final product that came after an indefinable amount of struggles. Hence, the cornerstone that gave them the tools for superiority are all secreted in the individual's heart and soul. Nevertheless, as humans continue to dream and achieve the impossible, all who seek to become more will endure and their willingness to pay the price for seeking the world of unknown possibilities will be tested. These fundamental steps are inevitable effects for anyone who seeks to upgrade or improve. It is something that must continuously cycle, just as the Earth rotates on its axis around the sun. And while most will only dream and ponder on becoming more, there will always be next breed who will rejuvenate the never-changing evolutional progression and its potential. It's just a matter of who will become the next victim of Mother Nature's unrelenting tests on the capabilities of human flesh.

Soul (spirit)

Lastly, the existence of the soul is, and forever will be, the most controversial component to prove, not only in humans, but in other living things as well. Since soul is something intangible, unlike the body and mind, it is something that cannot be shown to truly exist, and since all things in the physical world are manmade, everything from the abstract to intellectual things in life are subjected to being flawed and imperfect, no matter how educated and worldly a person presumes to be. The existence of soul will always be controversial, and whether it really exists or not will only be relevant or have any significance to an individual's beliefs in valuing their way of living. As with all things of life, it gives the human race something to fathom and think about.

The soul is just another mystery to occupy and justify human lives toward other possibilities and differentiate them from the rest. To say humans are better and given a greater sense of value and importance is just how an individual perceives to understand themselves as a being. Although humans have progressed and created what seems to be more complex socialization skills and expansion, they are far from understanding the true virtue to obtaining wisdom. Hence, whatever opinion an individual has on the existence of the soul is based solely on life experiences. It may give them inclination toward moral beliefs and put some kind of value on life having greater worth and meaning, but it's merely human-made doctrine in which to give more volume to already prejudiced and judgmental ideas. And although true and conclusive answers toward the existence of soul will be a never-ending debate, the impact and influence it has had on human development and an individual's climb toward the unknown depths of impossibility has provided more benefits and fulfilled its intended purpose more than finding concrete evidence in which to prove its existence.

The human race acts and thinks according to its genetic makeup, and they can't help themselves from wanting to understand. Because of this automated instinct or preordained characteristic in form of flesh, they are forever on a journey of conflicts between the known and the unknown. Therefore, within their philosophical mission to find out and want more justification for existence, they are forever searching within themselves for what best explains. Although in physical life humans have been branded to represent something greater than any other life-form, the flesh has a need for explanation. Hence, the question everything that exists must have a soul is just another occupying element to keep humans from boredom or decaying in motivation and vision. In turn, it's really not about whether certain things are true or if they've truly existed, like biblical stories to religious spiritual figures, but rather the imprint of stories gives beings something to fathom and give them inspiration that the impossible can be achieved within vulnerabilities.

Through history and ever-changing evolution, the quest to find conclusive answers to historical relics and doctrines which solidifies humans as something special has driven certain individuals into unknown depths. They are in constant conflict in their beliefs about life's meaning and purpose. Through these progressives, humans are in a constant search for something rare or unimaginable within the confines of flesh. Unfortunately, while they continue to put their greatest virtues and morals on one component, like that of soul, its value and degree of benefits can be as worthless as a decomposing corpse, because while some value themselves and even their domestic pets as sensitive beings, others live and exist as if they are just another irrelevant object that occupies space and time. To what degree and depth an individual finds their existence to be of greater worth all depends on the well-being of the self. Hence, whether humans or other species contain a soul is only relevant to an individual's sensitivity toward their existence.

Human curiosity in the cause and effect of worldly things to what is beyond is nothing more than trying to figure out all the beautiful crimson light in a crystal ball. Hence, there would be no end to the search beyond the flesh except within the abstract things of the metaphysical world. Because of this, humans will forever be in constant indifference within cultural beliefs. Nevertheless, the conquest of whether the soul exists in humans or any other living form will not only keep the interest in the discovery of wonders, but it will be responsible for shaping and molding the human species into civil and dignified beings, not only in society as a whole but more importantly individuality.

When something is created or developed, it takes a lot of energy in effort and persistence. One of the greatest examples of such a feat comes from a biblical story, where all living things and the universe were created within a certain amount of time, and because of the great amount of power that was needed for creation, the final day was given toward rest and recuperation. Although the spiritual stories may be left for debate, scientific reasoning understands the amount of time that was needed for all the planets, stars, and everything on earth to be created. There's no argument as to the estimation and intellectual evidence that the creation of life and everything else took billions of years. Through this analyzation, anything that is made must use a certain amount of energy. Otherwise, the intended goal or mission will be short-lived. Therefore, as humans proceed to extend and reach for whatever intrigues them, they are constantly challenged by obstacles and unexpected circumstances that may prohibit them from overcoming and achieving.

There are many avenues in both idealistic and practical things that humans feel the inclination to go forth and discover, and the specific means and purpose may be irrelevant, because within the population and the appetite of need and desire, the avenue of wanting to be and become is merely the fundamental survival tool to find their distinct position in life. Therefore, the purpose of the individual journey to become is not the ultimate question and conquest of justification, but rather the distance, time, complications, and suffering that will finally help them prevail over desolation.

The human drive to be is conditioned, whether it comes from the heart or an unknown place in flesh. They must produce energy of great proportions in determination to withstand complications. As all things must have progressive stepping stones when climbing to achieve, when a being of flesh who has the tools of mind to obtain and aims to fulfill an inner ambition "to be" attempts to accomplish something, they must fundamentally sacrifice and endure an indefinable amount of unpleasant situations while learning and earning a more acute sense of awareness in skills and capability. The problem is it's always easier to dream and wish to be than actually walking the miles and overcoming various obstacles. Whatever high level of achievement an individual seeks, whether physical, mental, or spiritual, they must inevitably endure and overcome their worst adversary of deformities within unpredictability. Because while needs and wants may be easily dreamt and desired, the reality in pursuing and achieving are an all-or-nothing kind of mission that will either make the individual become better or be forsaken into deterioration or destruction. And while questions may arise as to what makes some succeed while many fail, such as what level of determination and production of energy do they have that others cannot produce or imagine, these inquisitions will always separate individuals that have outperformed and stand out amongst the masses from the short-lived.

All humans contain the same structuring as fellow competitors. Although they may have different development and ideologies, all humans have the same components in internal and external physiology. But in the sense of achieving or failure, there's a fine line as to who has the greater will or determination to attempt going beyond expectations. While there always will be a great number who admire and desire to be, only certain fated individuals will become, while many others who sought and had the same desires and determination fade away into distant shadows and become another building block in the background of society. While there's a certain degree and level of determination to produce the energy and willpower to achieve an intended goal, the question is what's the difference and what do the acclaimed have that others don't.

All ambitions come from internal force, like the heart or instinct, but the degree of energy and amount of willpower needed to withstand the sacrifices and be persistent in continuous attempts and failures, being willing to endure more pain and struggles, must come from something deeper. Every individual feels that they truly want to be better and will give all they have from heart and soul. Unfortunately, because humans are flawed in natural state, depending on upbringing and discipline, they don't recognize the level of persistence needed. Therefore, as they attempt in a particular craft in which they will have to experience and endure indefinite amount of trials and tribulations, it will profoundly test their convictions. And while many will prevail in several years, eventually they'll be defeated by the constant pressures of trying to survive while working toward superficial success and notoriety.

The trials and perfecting of an individual craft are not the most crucial or difficult obstacles to overcome. Rather, it's the financial resources and depriving the needs of the flesh, like social interaction or personal addictions. While certain individuals will have support, unfortunately that is the most negative aspect of learning the true trades and skills of becoming something superior. Nature will intervene by making individual lives complicated through conflicts and unexpected situations. In trying to become something greater, there is one specific criterion that is done independently, without help from anyone or anything, and because of this and an individual's financial capabilities in which to provide for themselves, it's only a matter a time before most give up. In the real world of human survival, there are things that create constant financial pressure, such as having shelter, materialistic things, food, etc., and because crafting skills and fulfilling unorthodox dreams are sacrificed for an indefinable amount of time, years to decades or even a lifetime, maintaining livelihood in particular style becomes too much of a burden to withstand. In turn, the individual will either succumb to being like everyone else in society by getting a paying job or partner up with someone to play house. Either way, the daily needs for survival destroy most attempts to become greater, but a few rare ones are willing to sacrifice a bit longer in suffering in hopes of a better future.

The drive and motivation of one who succeeds must contain a different kind of energy source than others. While it's hard to measure and detect the tangible substance in production of energy compared to willingness to persevere, to achieve and succeed, there must be a certain depth of determination that has more intensity than others. To give some kind of reasoning or justification of how certain individuals overcome their worst adversary to prevail, the answer must lie within their soul. The heart, where most humans describe the virtue of the willingness to express true intent, is the place where they direct the feeling of inner vitality. Unfortunately, within the human desire to succeed, they are limited in degree of willingness to withstand the constant pressure of failure to maintain focus and discipline.

The success of individual's mission mostly depends on how they were conditioned from birth and development. Simply, if individuals were raised in a comfortable living conditions, like never going hungry or have a home full of love, then the odds of becoming something superior will be short-lived, because the main element that is required to become a greater being is coming from a suppressed or broken upbringing, where love and comfort is unrecognized. Therefore, any that stands out in society as the representation of a greater being has usually arisen from the darkened depths of deprivation, which gives them stronger motives and reasons to prove themselves of greater worth than what nature had given them; they were left out in cold and isolated but somehow overcame the most impossible of circumstances. And while many have failed because of the real harsh conditions of enduring and surviving in years of a suppressed life, through those misfortunes, life gave them the great powers of perseverance and determination in willpower because they had nothing else in life to uphold or cherish except death itself. While all forms of living contain some kind of energy, there are only a few who will understand and cherish their existence of being something of greater worth than just sustaining the functions of life. In turn, their willpower and determination to become better has more potency and vitality than a normal heart could ever pump or produce, and the power source must come from somewhere deep within their soul and spirit.

To Become Superhuman

Civilization is a platform, and all living things are participants in the big story of the human race. While there may be endless ideologies and infrastructure in the cast of humans displaced in different social class, for a few, it's a place where they can become something rare, in fulfilling internal ambitions. While they use various kinds of apparatuses and specialized talents to create a world of imagination in the movies, in the earthly realm, the stories and characters have limits and vulnerabilities in which billions play and act in designated places. And while most will only be seen as the building blocks in the background, some will become the blueprints from which books and movies are made and given recognition toward human's greatest accomplishments and failures.

Humans are conditioned within certain reforms, from earliest development to whatever age they live, no matter the cultural race. While there may be extreme of social conflicts between the rich and poor and prejudices in comparing good lives to bad, they all go through the fundamental phases of what is considered the human lifestyle by having some kind of home and relationships. Whether individuals live lives of luxury in loving households or are in a refuge from the desolation of the streets, through the generosity of invisible people or charities, they all have common things that they'll go through in finding daily necessities, like refueling their system by eating or finding amusement. However, no matter what style or level of comfort an individual was raised in, whether in chaos or pleasurable, they are all subjected to being conditioned and influenced to live in accordance with society.

Through nourishment and characteristics of interest or distaste, human physiology is preordained to transform into particular functions in which to give some kind of order. This cycle continues repetitiously as the children themselves become parents and until the end of life. Through this reproductive and development in adaptations, all humans believe and act, or are even manipulated, to maintain a certain level of responsibility toward life's intricacies, and whether they were born into misfortunes or blessings, they will all fit into and occupy some place within the vast landscape to continue the motion of civilization. While most will represent and become just another connective helix sequence in the social structure, never to be recognized beyond their importance to family and friends, others will become the main attraction in which society will be influenced or become the victim of amusement. At the same time, observers can only dream of being amongst the exceptional that seem to shake and disturb the balance of the old and bring the world into a new era of advancement.

Anything that is envisioned or dreamt can become real, no matter how obscure or uncharacteristic the idea may seem. In fact, all things abstract or unconventional ideas and visions have eventually become reality, especially if there was desire and the financial resources to create it. And whether the images were animations, realistic portrayals of superhero characters, or personal stories, all things came from first seeing the image from real life scenarios or nature's creations; without the visual illustrations and perception, nothing new would ever be produced. Nevertheless, whether the imagery comes from visions or the abstract things of nature, all things will eventually surpass their distinct time of need. While the physiology of the human race gradually progresses and ever increasingly manifests into a more perfected species of beings, the consequences and price paid in the duration of the sacrifices, pain, and struggles are never recognized as part of the bargain.

No matter what kind of life is lived, there's some form of negative or misfortune to both the privileged and suppressed, and everyone has to endure a certain degree of pain and struggles toward growth and improvement. But in wanting to be of greater worth and reinventing themselves, pain and struggles will be their greatest ally or adversary. When an individual seeks to be something superior, any mental, physical, or even spiritual suffering should be welcomed with open arms. The more they are forsaken within society and have to endure every trial and tribulation in physiology that they encounter, those elements will propel them onto the pathway toward potential successes; most importantly, they learn the skills of superior adaptability and being exceptionally corrigible in conflicts and difficulties.

Because of the human need for nourishment, emotional bonding, and everything affiliated with pleasure, if an individual was brought up and conditioned in easy and comfortable surroundings, training and disciplining for a greater cause will be a lot more difficult to endure. While humans often have self-pity from unfortunate upbringings, like lost souls who felt the cold of abandonment or neglect in social affiliations, these negative aspects of life become the greatest benefit toward training. The early introduction to emotional despondence and isolation makes it a lot easier for them to handle and have stronger convictions compared to those who were nourished. In the journey to becoming exceptional, many require loneliness and a nothing-to-lose attitude, which means they have nothing to distract them from intended goals. While there will always be individuals who achieve superior abilities through love and support, they will only be for a limited period of conditions, but for the lonely and suppressed, it is their one and only chance to raise themselves from the depths of darkness. They will pay the price or suffer any consequences in the hope to become something better and promising.

To become and achieve the impossible is not the most difficult aspect of the journey to manifestation; it's the time of length in loneliness while constantly trying to fulfill daily and personal needs and obtain the necessities for living. While most will be able to handle a few or more years of independence while striving for their goal, when it reaches decades of isolation and never getting any assistance or support from others, individuals are in danger of being destructive, especially if they're corrupt and have been conditioned within a life of privilege. There are many who have achieved more than they expected in just a handful of years, but that is nothing more than achieving a superficial level, with limited feats of superior abilities. They will come and go like a revolving door, and their future will become nothing more than just another example of many has-beens, where they sit in some place of refuge and reminisce about their past achievements. These individuals usually come from comfortable upbringings surrounded by emotional support to friendships. Although they have achieved or triumphed within a certain amount of time of dedication, because of the metaphysical strain of suppression and deprivation from a restricted lifestyle and constant and unpredictable economic shifts, the individual will only enjoy and live a brief moment of glory and eventually give up, deciding to just join the building blocks of society or, worst case, eliminate themselves from world completely.

Whatever particular area of expertise an individual has achieved beyond normal society standards, all their accomplishments should be given some kind of recognition and appreciated because of the price they paid and the sacrifices they made while enduring the obstacles toward self-growth. Whether they've achieved recognition in the media or sacredly within themselves, to overcome the darkened years of complications in persistence to not give up is something that can never be expressed or taken notice of until the individuals have accomplished their goal. There is no logic behind any particular ambition, because whatever area they feel the need to excel in or want to become superior form was out of their control and internally coerced by nature's intent. For example, in the real world where financial rewards surely benefit, if an individual plans to dedicate endless years in training and crafting a specified skill, it would be more logical to choose an area with financial gain rather than the childish ambition and dreams of superficial things for notoriety.

If human physiology can be perfected or achieve highly developed skills in a couple of months or perhaps a few years, then there would be time to change course to other ventures.

Unfortunately, since the human biological clock gives them a limited time until death, there are only certain periods in which they have the chance to show their intended creativity. Therefore, if they have not achieved or gotten some kind of justification, then the time of dedication that was put forth was done for nothing. While they could have obtained a job with a salary that would have eased survival, they instead invested all their time on something that was nothing more than an advanced hobby or fascination. There is no judgment or prejudices toward any feats of superior skill; whatever ails or inspires them to accomplish, they will follow the natural order of existence. It's not about what particular interest they've invested their time in, whether they were good or bad, but rather they felt compelled to follow and complete it to the best of their ability. On the basis that through different perspectives there's no such thing as perfection in choice, the determination and persistence of drive is the barrier between success and failure. Hence, whatever extreme an individual puts toward effort and determination is really the testimony of will to having the ability to overcome and achieve. In turn, it's really not about what particular superior skill that is acquired, it's how far they were willing to go in completion of the mission.

The difference between achieving and failure is simply the amount of exertion in willpower that's produced. It has nothing do with an individual's size, race, culture, or intellect. In fact, the less knowledge about the technological world of information and level of intelligence, or even the imperfectly genetically structured, like the outcasts of society, the better equipped or clearer the mind and focus in which to achieve the impossible. Although human intellect through academics has done wondrous things for innovation and development, it has also dampened or closed the doors toward new pioneering visions. If an individual has excelled too high on logical rationalization or in calculative odds, where they don't see the potential of something happening despite it being improbable, they would never attempt a project, or they would give up a lot sooner than expected. Therefore, within the journey and of becoming something superhuman, where the word itself is not logical, individuals must retain the naivety of a simpleton to want something illogically comprehensible.

To become something rare and unique is not for everyone, but many will attempt it, and through a lack of belief their mind and soul will not be opened or have the potential to handle and withstand the journeys ahead. This is the main factor in being something superior, because while society exists with a certain flow of energy, but for the rare and extreme, their energy frequency has no bounds and is intensified more by determination. Although this may be easily said, during the journey and experience of becoming a greater being, the sacrifices while withstanding the constant pressure, the relentlessness of confusion, and an almost bipolar mode of self-destruction will ever be rampant. Hence, the individual will have a never-ending conflict about if the price paid was really worth it, whilst envying common society for its naive security, because its price and the consequence of its existence seems a far cry from their own fate.

As the human race continues to revolutionize and manifest itself into better and stronger beings, it will succumb to the inevitable obstacles, challenges, and situations in which to strengthen means of survival while becoming something of greater form. Therefore, while civilization and mass society evolve and flow in constant motion with mynute changes, but there are a few who are forever fated to be something abnormal and overcome impossible odds to transform themselves into greater specimens.

Energy

Everything in existence is made from energy, whether it's a living, something abstract, or the gaseous molecules in the air that we all must rely on for life. While experts who have studied the metaphysics of the universe and earth may have some understanding in the geometric aspects of everything that exists, common people, and even college graduates, may have limited comprehension of the depth and complexity in the developing process of energy particles in matter. Nevertheless, all things are made from matter that contains energy, and although the human eye can't see it without high-tech equipment, it's unarguably the very foundation of all existence. This is why Confucius and other deep, philosophical religious doctrines says such things as everything from life to death transverses into one another as a continuous and never-ending cycle of regeneration, raising the idea of reincarnation and that all things are connected into one. In turn, there's no difference of beings made of flesh to other organisms, from the simplest to the most extreme.

Although human doctrine and ideologies in cultural indifference has created conflicts of interests that have caused chaos and destruction, unfortunately it's the fate of the human race to endure and overcome with some kind of resolution. Through ignorance and a lack of knowledge in understanding how everything is compounded in relatable form, especially within the diversity of human needs, creativity, and the ambitions to be greater, humans are merely victims of the never-ending cycle of incurable social conflicts. Nevertheless, as simplicity of energy can be altered and transformed, creating other definitions and explanations in the vast knowledge of unimaginable things, its existence and endless possibilities will continue to be a great mystery.

Through human cultural and ideological differences arose beauty and destruction within the same component of energy, and whatever way an individual sees and understands the process of creation, the practical truth for experts' how and what is at the core of all invisible molecules is conclusively the potential of power. The energy is in constant motion whether the object or living things are moving or not. Even in most dense substances in various elements and minerals, from diamonds to steel to chromium, that extreme heat can't melt, but within the core there's energy in motion. Although it may be easy to understand the mechanics of how energy in machines can be altered to increase and decrease power, within the human mind and body, the alteration of energy has more in depth of consequence than an individual would expect. In mechanical things, it's easy to change the frequency of energy and power, and if there is failure to simply adjust or get new parts. However, in human physiology, the increase and decrease of energy has certain consequences, which is simply the residue of exertion, but the cause and effect in ramifications can be life-threatening in mental deformities.

Everything in life, to outer limits of the universe, has energy in constant motion, and while control of the input and output are within the natural order, humans have influence over manmade objects and their own level of lifestyle and personal endeavors, where they can change and alter into more diverse or sophisticated beings. Through fundamental makeup and the natural order of creation, all things have a balance of good and bad. Hence, at the human metaphysical level, there's always some kind of negative aspects in whatever kind of life or relationships that they may evolve or expand. In turn, whenever they try to change or evolve themselves into other realms of possibilities, it causes discomfort and instability within accustomed lifestyle. Nevertheless, just as the makeup of the universe and everything that pertains to it must have continual combustion toward greater evolutional change, humans are no different, facing the same fate of demand in transversal effects. And since human structure is nothing more than coated molecules that embed the particles of energy, anything that is done within human physiology is coerced or manipulated by the speed and frequency of preordained motion that will entail same repercussions.

Human physiology can be dissected into unlimited combinations in an array of areas that represents their well-being and level of sophistication. In turn, it's impossible to decode any individual's energy level of its potential for success or failure. Human characteristics cannot simply be categorized in certain distinct placement of capability, because it's a lot deeper than just the dimensions of physiology. It's so diverse and far more complex than finding biological gene sequences. In understanding this, whether an individual is rich or poor or has passed or failed academics, there are no grounds to predict the stats to show the given level of energy contained. Because humans affiliate within the surrounding and constant interchangeable intricacies in the dispersal of energy, like doing things to maintain livelihood, in turn they only produce and disperse small bits of energy and rarely show extreme production in performances. This is why certain famed physicists once said that humans only use a very small percentage of mental energy capacity, and if they were ever to use just a little bit more, they would greatly excel and become geniuses in a particular field.

As humans continue to perfect themselves by achieving an array of things through skills and abilities, within the internal core of matter and mental ability there lies differences in the speed and frequency of energy that is in constant motion that is responsible for their disposition and placement within the social structure. And whether individuals are of high status or in a low class of irrelevance, it really doesn't matter, because on the basis that all things must have some negativity in struggles and pain, success and failure, every species on the land or the sea, even vegetation, are all participants in one big stage performance.

The drive or accelerator of human energy basically comes from three human components: mind, body, and spirit. Within these combinations arises diversity in which an individual will produce the will to be. Unfortunately, while they desire to learn how to obtain the powers of superiority, because they been conditioned by their environment and educated in the rationalization of realism that fiction is an impossibility, most importantly being raised and surrounded in artificial and fabricated homesteads, their physiology is limited in exertion of effort and determination. Although they might be in pursuit of becoming better with all their might, wholeheartedly giving best efforts with both mind and soul, because they were raised in certain confines restrictive to development, they're limited in ability to go beyond the norm. One such example is an athletes who tries to achieve the superior skills of a wild species but never comes close. Even though humans have achieved and revolutionized abilities in international games and records, their skills and abilities are still far from that of other primitives. It doesn't matter what kind of extreme physicality, competition, or accomplishments they have, the human ability to go beyond amongst other species is greatly limited.

Energy never dies or lessens in production, no matter the passing of time, but because of certain confines or lack of vision in determination, most are limited in attempts to be and obtain superior personifications. Every mobile species on Earth basically have the same internal organs, except for some rare adaptational adjustments, whether the species is wild or human, they all contain common components that are responsible for functions and continuous existence. Unfortunately, because of the differences in upbringing, development, food, and the environment in which they function, the levels of energy production in the physiological makeup are totally different. Because of this, wild species will always effortlessly dominate any physical contest, while humans would have to dedicate years to decades in training just to obtain a fraction of the wild species' ability. Therefore, while primitive species produce and act naturally and use superior skills in daily survival, humans, in the attempt to show greater abilities within the boundary of restricted conditions, where daily survival did not depend mainly on extreme physiology, produce dispersed bits of energy in labor and personal interests while living in a comfortable environment.

The potency of energy is strongest in its natural and raw form, so if the living things are left within nature's accord and not to be restricted in their journey, it will contain stronger energy because of its primitive survival instinct. If any living thing is conditioned and constricted in its development to associations, it will contain lesser potency of power. That is why domestic animals will always be weaker and less likely to beat any wild species in a contest of physical dominance. Although the domestic animals do have ability far greater than trained athletes, because they have been conditioned in environment of comfort and love, they have been corrupted and their natural abilities tainted. If domestic animal were left out in the cold to fend for themselves in the competitive arena of the jungle, their odds of surviving would be a lot less than if they had been born into the cold and isolation amongst other primitive species. While the reason and purpose of an individual's pursuit of superior ability will lie within personal prerogatives, at the same time, they are merely fulfilling their distinct order and displacement within social structure. Therefore, the logical reason why certain individuals would spend their life on an illogical activity and interests striving for a particular thing can only be defined by fate and destiny.

If an individual were given conscious choice of what powers and superior skills that they would like to possess, it would basically come down to things that would make their daily more profoundly atonable, such as making money and getting the best of lifestyle experiences without financial burden or repercussions. While certain individuals will proclaim to be more righteous or noble in way of life, like nothing related to money or self-gratification, nevertheless, whether individuals want to obtain superior abilities to do good or not, eventually every individual is naturally susceptible to being corrupted. In turn, the once-upon-a-time naivety and ignorance of not knowing their inner beast's appetite, they will recognize themselves as being sinful in the ways of gluttony. While wild species will often show their natural way of existence by dominating the weak and overindulged appetite while feeding if it weren't restricted by the natural order, humans would be no different in reaction and giving into natural instinct for fulfillment.

In the array of avenues in which humans could and would want to use superior abilities, within the control of the natural displacement of human dispositions and conditions in upbringing, there are automatic concessions in wanting to have a family, stable financial resources, or basically finding easily adaptable companionship. Hence, it's really not about choosing the type of superior skills and what distinctive way in which the power is used toward particular feats, because within the natural order of selection to a particular purpose of existence, distinct superior skills will all be chosen on the basis of being opposite to suppression. For instance, if an individual were poor, they will chase superior financial ability, and one who didn't seem to struggle will usually strive toward superficial fame or notoriety. Nevertheless whatever particular area or specialized superior ability an individual aims for and obtains, and whether their reason or purpose is consciously recognized or not, or even the time and dedication put forth had attained some form of compensation is irrelevant. Because all whether important or insignificant, are merely blueprints in which the next recipients can give their own assessment in which to think about toward prospects and ambitions. In turn, no individuals are wise or folly in a particular choice for superior abilities, because all feats of accomplishment or failure give possible avenues to future generations in direction or reinventing into better and perfected ways in which lives can be lived.

Training

Every specialized skill in human physiology needs to be disciplined to train and focus on intended goals. Whether it's something calculative of mind, the building of physical structure, or even to obtain higher spiritual awakening of inner self, the individual must condition their mind, body, and spirit into connective components, and hopefully with perseverance and willpower, they will prevail and overcome the impossible. In every era, back to the earliest time of existence, there always have been some who were exceptionally skilled within society, and as the population increased and human physiology advanced, there came other avenues in which humans achieved that were unconventional. In turn, they became something of a rare specimen to be admired or represented as a godly figure, sometimes even seen as a freak of nature. Nevertheless, in whatever way humans have revolutionized in genetic makeup and advanced themselves to the degree in which they have shown great feats of superhuman ability, by being conditioned in a humanistic way, they have merely broken the barriers in which to perfect themselves.

Therefore, even though humans have shown and recorded unbelievable showmanship and uncanny and innovative ways in using their genetic makeup to accomplish unimaginable things, because they've trained within the human condition, they've barely touched the surface in potential. Whatever level that has been achieved in great feats of challenge and overcoming obstacles should be respected and given some kind of appreciation for the dedication and sacrifices that were put forth. And whether they are recognized or obtained, superficial successes shouldn't really come into conflict with admiring and respecting the element of passion and dedication required.

Nevertheless, as humans advance and metamorphosize into more perfected beings, there must be more intensity and degree of sophistication in how they train and discipline in reach for superiority. That'll make previous imprints pale in comparison but give other pathways to achieving the impossible and a new sense of becoming something rare.

Achieving superhuman abilities is not as hard as the populous may perceive. Rather, obtaining higher levels of skills is easy compared to enduring the repetitive training and isolation time that is required to sharpen discipline. The power of ability and skills can be used toward whatever area an individual wish to expose in both productive and destructive influences, but the possibility that they can excel in creativity and inventiveness is endless. While those naive may believe that life should be perfect and has one pathway for fulfilling the appetite of need, realistically, the capabilities that have been conditioned can be used toward any particular interest. Whether the individual seeks the power of superiority toward a good cause or personal grievances, the journey and pathway in which to obtain the superior ability will have the same fundamentals.

Human life has become a lot more diverse and sophisticated since earliest of times, and existence is not all about just fulfilling the daily requirement of food or maintaining moral ethics and living righteous lives. Therefore, although humans have achieved an array of accomplishments in whatever degree of recognition or irrelevance, because human accolades and the intensity level of exploits are prejudiced in what is acceptable or not in the moral standards of society, there are only certain and foresighted things that may get the recognition or justification. By being controlled by unpredictable hormones, human have different reasons and purposes for wanting greater skills and abilities. Therefore, while it's an easy admission for the superior ability to be righteous so that morally good things are accomplished, when the greater skills have negative aspects, where the individuals have used a specialized ability for selfish needs and gratification that caused chaos and destruction, then the feats are never recognized as being great achievements, even though the investment of time and isolation in trials and tribulation may have been the same.

The power and energy inhabited within human physiology can be used negatively or productively. Although society seeks and fights for peace and tranquility, unfortunately its nothing more than naivety and ignorance of how an individual sees the real world and the inevitable necessity of conflicts from the simplest things in life to the universe coexisting with opposite entities. While the conditioned human mind will bicker and debate over what justifies a superior level of abilities and how the power of creativity should be used, within emotional traits of possible compromises in enduring and the impatience of tantrums in trying to justify rightful claims, constantly struggling within unpredictable opportunities, what and how an individual choose to subside or corrupt themselves in personal endeavors to survive can only be answered within their distinct order of displacement in the vast maze of life. Hence, every individual is just a particle of matter that is showing and representing the possible ways humans can construct into other dispositions. And whether they play and act the part in personification of good, bad, or any other, there's always somebody who's going to fit into the missing gaps, filling vacancies of productive and destructive. Therefore, in reaching for greater powers, individuals have the right to spend their one and only life in the flesh how they see fit.

There are many ways to train and gain discipline in an array of areas. While the human way of training may consist of assistance, financial support, or boosting self-esteem, those are humanly conditioned ways and far from the superior method of self-reliance of independence like the earliest pioneers. Therefore, when wanting to be exceptional beyond human understanding, the journey and training will have to be done alone, assisted only by experiences and by constantly evolving themselves by observing and learning from surroundings and adaptation to different situations within the never-ending pursuit. It's an automated instinct of conditioned development that humans have in wanting assistance and having some kind of support toward goals and ambitions because of being corrupt in their accessibility to resources. While most will have avenues of help through friends and associates, they will be the weak link that may prevent them from achieving the greatest of possibilities. Even if the individual did have some kind of support in finance or motivation, the question is how long it will be before the individual becomes too much of burden because of the constant financial dependency and emotional turmoil, especially in ups and downs of pressure and expectations, because supportive people and friends have their own lives and responsibilities without adding the constant and unpredictable economic stress.

The journey to become greater is like a Russian roulette game; the individual must have a mindset of being willing to sacrifice and give up the safety net of security and the common comfortable lifestyle. Anything that is above or not within the norm of society should not be attempted, because to become something of an extremist is not for the faint of heart. Rather, it's for who has nothing to lose but life itself, which would be nothing short of a blessing in disguise. While there always will be examples of those who have succeeded by assistance and emotional support from family and associates, they are nothing more than those who accomplished superficial feats. Hence, they will have their moment of heightened sense of superiority, and then wither away in an abyss of once upon a distant memory of what has been. But whether an individual becomes someone with superior skills in particular crafts or artistry or just have touched the surface of heightened senses, it really doesn't matter. All things will eventually die, and trying to reminisce upon what once was is nothing more than illusory perception in a hormonal state of mental psychosis. Therefore, it's really not about climbing the highest mountains or fulfilling a bigger appetite of need; it's about accepting one's destiny and finding some kind of solace in the journey, in turn creating other pathways in which to teach future generations a new sense of possibilities.

It doesn't matter what part of human physiology an individual wants to improve, whether it's for reasons of financial gain, some kind of imprint in recognition, or even simply self-exalting in knowledge and wisdom, the training will have the same intensity and discipline. Unfortunately, it can cause emotional damage to an individual's well-being because of the loneliness and continuous uncertainty, not having a clear direction toward the intended mission. As each year goes by with the never-ending twists and turns in obscurity without resolve, the level of determination and withstanding the irritation of the monotony takes its toll. As such, the mental condition can change because of the deprivation of human companionship and the lack of success, burning out self-esteem, which could easily lead to a more destructive state of mind. Either the mental distortion and continuous suppressive life causes one to become productive or destructive, where simple things like venturing to your job or eating will become too much of a burden. In turn, the individual is now left out in the darkness of no return, where even common ways of social involvement seem irrelevant. It would be easy to escape into the world of various substances like alcohol or narcotics, which could last indefinitely.

Through history there have been many with potential who succumbed to destructive behavior and never reclaimed normalcy. They became lost souls in the maze of life. Unfortunately, it continues, never having a shortage of victims as others try to obtain godly secrets. In these phases, the triggering of self-destructive behavior will be very near reality in thought and may lead to unethical behaviors or alternatives in either continuing or ending it. Although this may seem unfathomable toward progress, it is a necessity in which to show the one that is destined to be and the one who overestimated themselves into a goal to reach the unattainable. These incidents of uncertainty sometimes occur in rotational cycles, daily or monthly, and sometimes are unpredictable. Hence, it can seem like a dead end without any resolve after uncountable years invested toward a vision.

While it may seem that Mother Nature has cursed or condemned the individual with this continuous, suppressive misdirection or manipulation, it is merely the greatest of lessons to be learned and experienced, because becoming something exceptional cannot be done with just a few conventional obstacles or challenges. Rather, everything from employment to living quarters must continuously change, and the more things the individual gets involved in adjusting the better it will be toward reaching superiority. While others sit in comfort and stagnation, for the fated one, resting and having security become limitations in evolving themselves into something rare. When enthusiasm and willpower slowly deteriorate, having nothing to show for all the time and dedication put forth, enduring the most extreme living conditions for a long duration, where everything from daily nutrition to living quarters were no better than what prison inmates or even stray animals have been accustomed.

Through these situations the individual's dreams and ambitions are continuously shortened, and the trigger finger ever increasingly tightens to release themselves from cursed fate that was once thought of as an honorable mission in which to justify rightful claim to obtain the godly powers of superior abilities. Nevertheless, as humans revolutionize into a new advanced species, there will be price and consequence that must be paid. Otherwise, the most dominant species that is predestined to change the natural order for greater prosperity will become stagnate and not able to evolve, from the complexity of the mind to simple genetic structure, into new forms. Therefore, while the majority of society will maintain its natural existence within the same frequency of energy, there will be others who will be coerced to change original state into a greater representation. In turn, they will journey into unknown abyss in which to satisfy their ever-lingering instincts and greater ambitions to awaken themselves from the deep sleep of the subconscious.

The training will begin when an individual has chosen particular goals and interests with the intended thought of submitting to discipline. The individual should have a logical understanding and make a conscious choice to enter into a suppressive lifestyle. While this extreme condition in which to train the mind and body in discipline can be used in all sorts of ways in obtaining greater skills and abilities, it's best suited for serious and deep, subconscious thought processing in which to gain a better understanding of vision. This includes how to do things better, rather than using the power for casual interests, like using various physical attributes as gimmicks. Nevertheless, with a higher and more intense level of energy, they have the choice of how best to use the power source. If the individual lives an extreme suppressive life in isolation and depravity, it would not be beneficial or logical to do it just to perform childlike tricks rather than logical and calculative metaphysical skills.

To start the process, they must detach themselves from all associations with family, friends, and even technology. If this first part cannot be met or considered, then their attempt to reach superior form will be interrupted, and failure lies a short distance away from the intended mission. Although there are countless examples of who have achieved this through the love of friends and family. Unfortunately, those are superficial achievers, a socially conditioned moment of glory, because true superior abilities are not recognized within glamorized world. The fine line between an individual who has touched and felt the moment of superiority in a commercial way and the one who stands out and comes closest to being superior have differentiation from being in the spotlight and being hidden from public view.

A true superior being lives a life of uncertainty and loneliness from comfort, isolated from places of endearment. Through this they will obtain a greater sense of ability and skills. If the individual wants to achieve the human-conditioned version of superior form, seeking glamour and admiration, then being surrounded and praised in motivation and support is the pathway. But if they want to make an exceptional imprint, then they must condition themselves in seclusion in which to become the best in a particular field. In a lifestyle of privileges with the emotional embodiment of love and living in a colorful environment, it's nearly impossible for them to endure a certain form of environment in which to discipline and train. All human acclaim and successes in whatever degree and depth that are socially achieved may be looked at as being something superhuman, but very few will ever uphold and maintain their status for an indefinite time. Most will eventually succumb to falling back to reality by taking part in the molding of society and relaxing in comfort. Therefore, while the emotional bonding of friends and family is important and will give support in tough times, unfortunately the isolation and detachment are small but necessary sacrifices that must be adhered to as a stepping ground in which to enter the world of superhuman.

While losing emotional support may be hard enough, other important things must be given up or adjusted to are living without materialistic things, gadgets, and living in luxury with all kinds of decorated accessories to beautify the interior, like fancy furniture. They may be in presence of it unintentionally or briefly, but because of constant moving and the unpredictability of life's endeavors and the need for continuous evolving and experiences, all material and superficial things become nothing more than distractions and unnecessary burdens. Therefore, in reaching for extreme levels of skills and abilities, the individual in pursuit of that must be really desperate. In turn, they will be required and even coerced by nature in demanding giving up nothing short of all human desires by enduring the sacrifices during the transformation of becoming new and improved; the demise of conquering will be fated by their own determination.

While the initial willingness may easily be forthcoming by enthusiasm who are psyched to enter into the unknown of superior possibilities, especially when having some kind of financial support, eventually, through nature's intervention of causing unexpected complications in the teaching of lessons, the accessibility to resources will gradually dwindle, not so much because of expenditures in overzealous spending, rather through inexperience in using money for daily necessities. Hence, they'll go through financial problems and put themselves in dire straits. In turn, they must venture out into the world for money-making opportunities, and in whatever way the individual finds their refuge from the financial crisis will be their own prerogative, whether righteously or illogically. In desperate need of necessities like a place to live or finding food, an individual must find some kind of resource either by working or some other accessible reservoir. They can go to shelters, churches, or even scrounge legally or illegally, but it'll be uncomfortable. While society often looks down upon people who enter those kinds of places, for individuals who want to grow stronger and have better sensibility in wisdom, having experienced desolate social situations will have a greater benefit than always living in security. Although a logical and sensible way is to find an occupation, within the constraint of slow progress in endless, tedious hours of labor, either in time or jobs that come with low wages, the individual may eventually give up and turn to other avenues in which to obtain more beneficial financial compensation.

In real life, humans have been conditioned and are easily corrupted by flesh and hormonal indiscretions. Hence, they are not to be trusted as being subjective in crisis situations, as they are easily manipulated by emotional compromises. Because of this, although they may have full-hearted intentions of doing good and living in a righteous, moral way, but when confronted with a situation where their needs are constricted and suppressed, they can easily go from being well-adjusted to someone who acts illogically, forgetting their one-time strong beliefs. Therefore, when an individual is in dire straits in terms of securing daily necessities, which is an essential learning process, overcoming and enduring the repercussions will be the greatest challenge. It could be as simple as the need for food, to the extreme condition of dependency on addictive substances. During the lengthy time of uncertainty and the absence of emotional connections, it's inevitable that they will have other needs and means to put themselves in constant pressure of financial burdens that minimum-wage jobs cannot sustain.

While the initial conflicts were simply finding living quarters or having financial resources for daily survival, as time passes without resolution, the appetite for daily necessities changes the whole dynamic, which causes internal conflicts of interest regarding their mission and objectives. Whether individuals face the crisis and fall into the depths of darkness or are just going through the rituals and strengthen their character and increase awareness of life's pitfalls, only a few will come out alive. Many will enslave themselves for the mere pleasures of the flesh, and their ambitions and dreams will just be a glimmering light that got lost in the flames and buried in some distant memory. Whether the individual is within a certain group or in the isolation of reinventing themselves into a superior being, solitude and being distantly lost in thought will be paramount and an inevitable tribulation of mental deformities. Hence, while others and society may go about daily activities, the individual in pursuit of self-discovery will go into seclusion and continue makeshift of crafting skills.

It's difficult to say whether it's better to be involved and hide in social irrelevance in which to break from the monotonous or maintain a solitary of life in keeping the necessary tunnel-vision, because others will have prejudices about the dissociative alienation. For instance, within the process of having mental discipline, would being alone, rejecting companionship, and not being a participant in an organization be easier? Or would conjoining with others just to make the mental agony of loneliness less painful be better? While the pursuit may be hard enough, fighting against society's way of thinking and the peer pressure of living in the standard way with family and friends can distract and destroy the prospects for success in endeavor. There are a lot of obstacles and challenges that will be faced when individuals are in pursuit of greater self-improvement, so the degree of sacrifices and withstanding outsiders' watchful eyes and annoyance can deter them from intended goals. When isolated and independent, fighting against indifferences can be more easily confronted than if an individual were living and dependent on certain places and social affiliations because of wanting to attach themselves to resources. Nevertheless, within will and need to fulfill whatever ails them, there will be no other choice than to pursue their instinctive pathway of destiny. While the difficulty of challenges and obstacles will come within social situations, those are merely the tip of an iceberg compared to other conflicts that must be endured to withstand the monotony of being alone and isolated from normal standard of life.

The initiative was merely to envision a superior ideal of particular traits, whether superficially related or not. The next step is to find some kind of occupation that will help in survival and keeping physicality in motion. In most cases, the individuals who have great ambitions and dreams will come from those suppressed in self-esteem of having inferiority complexes, likes outcasts in society or those unequipped to succeed. These individuals would come from the social ladder of the uneducated and those deprived of opportunities, especially the socially inept or those with aggressive personality with limited potential. Because of that, their credentials for the workforce and salary placement will be little to none, especially if they have other drawbacks likes a criminal record or are marked within the negative aspects of society. Therefore, job choices are limited to almost nonexistent—not because they're not available, but lack of experience or education, or impatience, will leave them out hanging, possibly becoming a bottom feeder in society. Nevertheless, within that suppressed life, they should and will have the greatest potential in which to endure and have a never-give-up attitude compared to the privileged and educated.

Whether the individual comes from a good financial background or a deprived one, both have the energy of power within them to attempt achieving a goal, The problem is within the regimen of living a suppressed life and being deprived from social associations, it may have negative projections. So, if an individual comes from a good upbringing full of love and comfort, the odds of success are greatly lower than those who were socially deprived. Nevertheless, whatever social ladder may be attempted, they must obtain some kind of employment, though not just for financial reasons. Rather, being among common people and doing some kind of labor will give them the greatest tools and innovative ideas in which to advance and trigger the creative mind.

While there always have been and forever will be supposed superior beings in an array of human occupation, like various skilled experts to commercially made influences, who had not put in extensive mileage or worked very hard, they are merely superficial imprints of notorieties that will have their limited moment of glory. While higher-paying jobs will be more benefit to survival, the more slave-driving and low-paying occupations will unfortunately teach the greatest lessons in perspective toward advancing ingenuity. Because of these criterions in ethical things of independence and working under the conditions of the common citizen for the daily fundamentals, it'll just be a matter of time before the individual decides to give up or head toward self-destruction because of the continuous pressure and expectations over the years without any rewards or compensation. Through these extended struggles and the indefinable amount of time elapsed and yet to be endured, most conditionally born and raised in the love of the privileged will slowly detach. Hence, the ones that were looked at as genetically imperfect and the outcasts of society, without potential, will have best motive and production of energy in which to become something greater.

Food (nutrients)

All living species must have some kind of refueling system, edibles, in which to continuously rejuvenate and sustain life. While other organisms have their own specific methods of maintenance, a human's need for, and the variety of, nutrients has almost no limits. Unfortunately, they are conditioned to overindulge in endless ways that could corrupt and limit them in achieving superior physicality as they reach toward something exceptional. Although food intake is a must for all living things, when humans are seeking to take their body into superior performance and adaptability, the daily consumption of food could be a barrier to challenging themselves into achieving the impossible. The earliest nutrients were simple, proteins and vegetation, but as humans modernized with overpopulation, there came other avenues and new methods to create them. Even though most were naturally grown, humans have reinvented the natural creation for the specific pathway to feed the masses, but it has also created another pathway toward endless employment. Through innovative ideas to help find a greater sense of pleasure in food, humans have been corrupted by the excess indulgence, and when reaching toward greater sensibility in values and achieving superior form, they could easily be dampened or discouraged when enduring the journey because of the newly conditioned addictive needs.

Through the passage of time and evolutional changes, human physiology had to adapt and been endlessly challenged by both manmade and natural disaster, like ecological devastations, wars, and economic recessions that have caused more suffering than humans could have ever imagined. Although these events may have been difficult, through them humans have learned to overcome limited ideals and find a greater ability to adapt and grow in knowledge in which to evolve into an improved species to face toward future uncertainty. From the simplest of being able to survive economic repression in limited resources and job availability, to migration into unknown territories and the unpredictable trials and tribulations of the journey, in these times, both individuals and families had to endure an unaccountable amount of physical deprivations in hunger or starvation. Whether it was caused by ignorance or the unfortunate circumstances of natural disasters, humans of all ages, from the very young to the elderly, had to endure limited resources and famine in families, cities, and even nations. Unfortunately, humans will never be able to prevent the continuous suffering of malnutrition, because as each era came and went within its own level of suppression, it continues to be the ultimate fear.

In the meantime, as modernization develops with more availability, some will purposely challenge their physicality into new dimensions by taking the body into unknown boundaries in which to train and perfect ideal vision of superior form. Through visionary ideals in which to heighten the capability of their inferior physiology compared to the counterpart primates, humans have taken their vulnerable bodies to unknown heights. Most of it was in the purpose of sporting competition, but some challenge themselves unconditionally, for their own reason, by taking the physicality to extreme levels in calorie depletion, even malnourishment, causing possible self-annihilation. The reason and purpose may not be as important as showing the capabilities of such an inferior body, trying to conquer the impossible. Therefore, as human resources became more abundant, where most of the society gladly indulges, others attempt to become something of a rarity and endure extreme levels conditioning in physicality; many will attempt it, but few will prevail.

While there may be many methods for athletes to train, from nutrient deprivation to the perseverance toward a particular physical feat, some will take their body into extreme calorie deficiency, enduring internal complications that could affect internal organs and cause life-threatening predicaments. One example is long-distance marathon runners, who must only eat limited amounts and kinds of foods that will allow their body to perform for long periods whilst the body is constantly drained and demands more energy for performance. The stomach contents have long been drained of the nutrients, and the body then begins using muscle tissue as a continuous fuel source into other vital organs. If an average person attempted that athletic feat, they would surely collapse from exhaustion and organ failure, but after specific training and determination over a long period of time, certain athletes are able to perform and take their once very limited and vulnerable physiques to incredible heights.

Then there are other athletes who seek to obtain the physicality of cartoon characters, where the muscle mass and size is unrealistic, conditioned into hardness, like extreme bodybuilders who baffle observers with their freakishness. While most humans would be amazed at the size and weight of particular athletes, when fluid-celled forms become over-massed within a vulnerable, limited skeletal structure, then seeing and touching something that is transformed into the hardness and density of steel is something beyond comprehension. Nevertheless, while most logical and sensible observers would question the reason for this particular interest and investment, the depth and time in personal sacrifice, from financial to emotional complications, can never be understood, enduring calorie deprivation for an extensive time, years or even decades. Hence, the mental turmoil and self-preservation of believing oneself capable of obtaining that goal can never be truly appreciated, because as humans who have experienced nutrient deprivation to whatever degree, and seeing a certain individual who will endure it for decades and overcome it, they have shown the uncanny ability to conquer their vulnerable flesh.

Unfortunately, in reaching to become the truest superior form, above all superficial notoriety and recognition, these are the least of the challenges and obstacles that must be endured and persistently overcome in which to differentiate the individuals from other superior beings. Hence, what once were thought of as great feats of accomplishment, for the extremists or the most rare, the human method of obtaining and accomplishing will have no effect toward the journey and training in which to become something most supreme.

Even though humans conditionally believe they need to maintain and eat a certain amount of food daily, history and time have countless stories where certain individuals have shown that the human body can go without proper food, or none at all, for an extensive amount of time, in both conscious decisions or because of unfortunate situations, such as individuals who purposely put themselves in food deprivation through fasting as part of their religious beliefs, or individuals who got lost in some distant place without preparation of survival necessities. Some of those individuals showed they could survive without food, or even water, for days, weeks, and months. Even within the unfortunate and trying time of war and its cause and effect, people who were imprisoned or kept in seclusion for years, where daily nutrients were minimal to nonsexist, their skeletal structure could be seen through very tightened skin, but they survived. Although it may have been in the most undesirable circumstance, it showed the incredible, zealous spirit and will for humans to endure unbelievable predicaments without the presumed bodily needs. Therefore, although there are continuous complaints of modern humans who seek more food than needed, certain individuals have shown that humans can survive and adapt without daily nutrients.

As modernization has provided for an abundance of food, to the point of gluttony, to build the physicality into superior form, what society requires in daily nutrients will be limited or irrelevant in reaching that goal. For instance, as modern athletes develop all kinds of variations to physical stature and capabilities, they rely too much on excess nutrients and supplements. Although every athletic performer should be appreciated for their distinct ability and accomplishments, they are too dependent and vulnerable of being compromised with the unpredictable economic shifts and nature's cruelty. Hence, without financial resources in jobs and a support system, their feeling of being superior will become tainted. Therefore, when striving to become the truest superior form, the common way of developing and building physique will have to be eliminated.

Human physiology has incredible durability in its capability to adapt that continues to mystify the intellectuals, because in an array of every-day accidents, including life-threatening mishaps where vital internal organs have been badly damaged and the rest of the body has limited function, somehow many survive. Although showing the mechanics of building muscle fiber with limited food may not be of vital of importance, showing the depth to which the human body can store nutrients within cells that have long been absent of food is something to be marveled and appreciated. Because while common athletes usually eat before and after training with other foreign substances, to create a superior body, the individual must train without needs of food and must never care about any other substance whilst continuously producing the energy for exertion, and sitting down and relaxing will only be a brief moment of tranquility before bedtime. Although food intake will be at a certain time of day, it will never be in training or be the main concern after workouts, rather going to work and doing other things in which to progress toward the intended goal.

The human body does not need as much food as is presumed, like three meals a day or even more. That is why the human body produces so many bowel movements, because it cannot absorb or store the excess amount in the normal hormonal balance. Even athletes that produce high performances do not need as much as they consume. Hence, they will be hindered or inconvenienced with regular bathroom use that could severely interfere with daily personal affairs, but because they are so accustomed to the abundance and easy access, they will corrupt themselves with the unnecessary intake of food.

The blood cells have a special mechanism that stores all kinds of nutrients that will be used when most needed, so even if a person skips a meal or two within the day, the body has the ability to use the stored nutrients. This is why certain individuals have survived food deprivation for short to or even unbelievably long periods of time. Therefore, when training the body and using energy to build muscle fibers, continuous intake of nutrients is not required. Rather, it's the individual's willpower that produce the energy for performance, even in the case of limited nutrient resources. Although building muscle mass does require an increase in nutrients because it exasperates the muscle tissues irregularly while training, they will excrete large amounts of sweat through excessive eating or the intake of supplements. Eating does not give muscle fiber true density, because more volume in muscle mass means more weight in the form of liquid.

So, while there will always be many types and degrees of athletes, to be something rare and beyond the common, an individual must produce profound amounts of energy. Otherwise, no matter the acclaim or notoriety, they are just another superficial imprint compared to most advanced forms of human physiology.

Living Conditions

The living quarters of a trainee can be anywhere in the world, but being in the inner cities can have advantages in the availability of jobs and resources compared to a rural location. Although being in an isolated place in the countryside or even the outskirts of a city in a suburb is important for a greater level of focus, but extreme desolate areas could limit opportunities to learn and gain experience. One thing is for sure, the less decorated and more spacious it is, the better the flow of oxygen and the higher energy level the room will have.

Humans are conditioned to living in fabricated structures filled with all kinds of things to occupy space. Although it may be beautiful and homey, the percentages of energy and oxygen are limited, depending on how crowded the space is. For example, if the room is large, like those in big houses or even outside tents, there's plenty of good energy and oxygen. But when living in limited spaces crowd with all kinds of objects, which most humans have become accustomed to doing, then the energy level and oxidation are not as high. In turn, their mind functions within tedious technical occupations where they do same routine job for years, so daily life and activities at home will have same rotational cycle of dispersing of energy for personal interests and maintaining inner sanctums. It doesn't matter if they live in an apartment with small rooms, with some rearrangement and shifting of objects, a small room can get just as much energy and oxygen potency as oversized rooms. This is a perfect example why people who function at a higher mental level live in spacious living quarters, while the common worker with tedious jobs requiring minimal mind function live in small homes.

The location and size of the living quarters doesn't really matter, but the type of decorations and furnishings will have a great effect on well-being and the way the mind functions. When it comes obtaining a higher level of mental power, the condition of the interior of the home and how an individual occupies in daily activities is more important than the extravagance of the decorative. Even if individual were living in a space the size of a jail cell, there can be higher level of energy and oxidation than living in middle-class or lavish homes. It's just matter of changing or rearranging the interior furnishings and eliminating the unnecessary, most importantly, not being dependent on materialistic things and being able to adapt by accepting a certain degree of discomfort. Therefore, while in training to become something of greater form, an individual must be able to downsize in comfort to a minimal amount of things in living quarters.

In reach for the maximum level of power for performance, the individual must also adjust things likes their attire, home gadgetry, and how it is maintained in cleanliness, because as humans have evolved in the mechanics of adapting in society and dignifying themselves as being a better and more profound species, they have collectively decorated and manifested their own disguises in which to portray and distinguish individuality, not so much for vanity, but because civilization has rules and regulations about nakedness. Hence, everyone must wear certain outerwear so as to limit perversions and create civilized beings. Although there are a few rare freaks who would like people to run around naked, most logical and respectable people who understand the fine line between freedom of expression and the need to be dignified form would wear clothes even if there weren't laws and regulations. Because although the human species proliferates and is in a never-ending search to fulfill the appetite of inner beast with sexual intricacies, for the sake of safety and the proper edicts in developing future generations, there must be some kind of rationalization in understanding the importance and necessity of those laws and regulations.

For continuous existence and to exhibit superiority over other primates, humans must maintain a certain representation of civility. Therefore, in their array of domestic hang-ups and adapted customs, they must continuously rotate and cycle daily appearance and keep their homesteads clear of dust and filth. In doing so, a certain percentage of daily energy is spent on domestic chores like cleaning, cooking, laundry, etc. While there will always be some amount of the population who neglect tidiness, including high-functioning intellectuals who are at the top of their fields, like a famed composer Mozart and countless historical figures, the majority of population will accept and adapt to maintaining private sanctuaries, whether rich or poor and regardless of the social standing. So, most human daily energy is spent on fundamental survival, and when other things like kids and pets are added, the energy level is depleted even more. Since they only produce a certain amount of mental energy in which to handle all these tasks, in turn they will forever be known and accepted as a common member of society who has no special talent or extraordinary mental capabilities. Because they spend so much time on raising a family and taking breaks to relieve stress, work and hobbies or other personal addictions, they live day to day just doing tedious maintenance. They will wish to obtain greater things, but because they are locked into an automated system of daily rituals, they will never be able to make any drastic changes to finances or job situation until they make changes to the dynamics of mental discipline. Therefore, they must change their frequency of energy and oxidation in order to maximize potential ability to become something superior.

The individual in pursuit of discovery will attempt to train in their most comfortable place, not so much in luxury but within familiarity, like the neighborhood or around friends. They will do whatever they feel is necessary to put them on the pathway toward a particular field of enterprise. While nothing in life has a definite road or method for success, staying around the distractions of family and friends is of the least benefit. Nevertheless, through naivety and instincts, an individual will attempt to exceed certain parts of physiology toward the endeavor. In those times, the mind will be filled with enthusiasm, and nothing will deter them.

As a predictable species with an automated sense of preservation, humans are only prone to act and think when provoked, just like a cornered animal will only move when in danger. Humans are most especially easily coerced and manipulated to change if they're threatened by certain unequivocal situations, because out of all species, humans are evolutionally better equipped genetically with a sensitive value system and mechanics for survival. Therefore, whatever the situation, if there is a desire and will to live, they are the greatest proliferators in which to adapt and succeed in particular goals. And while they may feel that they can deprive and teach themselves the important lessons to be learned in taming their unhealthy habits toward growth, unfortunately, because they've been comfortably nourished in mind and body, they cannot teach themselves how to go beyond expectations and recondition themselves toward achieving greater abilities.

In attempt to train and become some superior form, a person will face unexpected situations that will create chaos, complication, and mental agony. And in these moments, the individual will be confused, not knowing which direction they should take to continue on with intentions. Depending on how much time they have invested toward crafting skill, the individual will be faced with decisions in which to confront their dilemma. While mental anguish and frustration have their own degree of suppression, the most depressive influence will come from constant daily financial pressure in securing the necessities. In these particular situations, the end may seem near, but if the individual has the will, they will not give up, continuing to pursue their goal. Eventually, with resource help from social structure like shelters and charities, there will be an outlet from the impossible situations. Although there is light at the end of every darkened tunnel, in the continual travel to search and find some glimpse of hope will lie within the control of natural order, but if not given up they will prevail.

While life-threatening situations, financial woes, and mental depression will create Armageddon-like scenarios, the old saying of what doesn't kill you will only make you stronger is the very key to learning the lessons from the most difficult challenges. Just as in the movie, Superman's powers were earned by traveling through different planets, for individuals to obtain acuteness of senses as those in a superior being, they too must constantly move and experience to obtain knowledge toward future endeavors.

While poetic words can create an illusory image of hope and understanding, unfortunately they are merely possible avenues to finding some support or tranquility in moments of despairs, but the impact and benefits are as distant as the sun is to the Earth. And if creative words can dispel the individual from taking drastic negative actions toward themselves on the road to self-destruction, the effect and change it'll have on the world will be as worthless and uninfluenced as removing one sand grain from the vast desert. When an individual has put forth years and decades toward ambitions and dreams and has endured countless amounts of loneliness and invested a profound amount of energy without any rewards or compensation, there are no words that can give some kind of solace. While others may see the sorrow and helplessness within the sunken soul, for individuals to find reserve sources of energy in which to continue on with life can only be defined by the deflated desire and drive.

Some naive and sympathetic bystander might suggest just cheering up and readjusting, or some old wise and experienced words might give some kind of preservation in a moment of tranquility as an attempted antidote for the deadly disease of feeling distraught, but as one ends life another is birthed, and this cycle will continue until the end of time. Therefore, even if an individual never looks at the lighter side of not fulfilling their intended ambitions, the world and everything in it will continue as if the individual was never born. In turn, the defeated have sacrificed and valued their one and only soul as being as worthless as other disposable objects that have no significance.

Everything in life has certain consequences. It's the very foundation and cornerstone in which all things are made, and when an individual is in search of a higher energy source, like godly powers, the ramifications will have a greater impact than any human conflict or complications imagined. Nevertheless, while most will never dream or dare to seek mythological and unimaginable ideals, there will be a few who will attempt to tame and achieve the impossible, and the true victor over failure will lie within an individual's way of understanding and perspective on life.

The main agenda and condition the individual must visualize enduring is simply eliminating all things that distract the energy flow from continual acceleration, likes social associations and personal hobbies. Although those two things are the main components that will limit obtaining superior ability, the daily financial pressures and withstanding a continuous suppressive life will create greater depth in complexity and intensity. Because the individual who seeks to manifest into a more perfected being will most likely not come from a warm and well-adjusted financial situation, the main cause and effect in the will of determination will come from a suppressive existence where hunger and desire are at their strongest. Nevertheless, the smaller the living space and the fewer distracting mechanical accessories the better and more befitting in conserving energy toward mission focus.

While the idea of a superior being seems like an impossible fantasy, there have always been historical examples, and it was never in failing or a lack of genetic makeup, no matter how perfect or imperfect humans are born and develop. Rather, because humans were conditioned in certain ways and had a lack of vision, it prevented them from becoming something superior. Therefore, while most of the population may lack in vision and comprehension that life is more than just family and friends, to become superior, they must look into other alternatives and metamorphosize themselves and become improved. Otherwise, the human race will never advance from its state of simplicity into something greater. So, while humans are conditioned to associate and live lives of automation full of distractive comfort, in the reach for a greater sense of self-reliance in strength and advancement, they must come to terms with living independently and dealing with the precariousness of insecurities.

While there are many skilled and exemplary individuals who have achieved beyond the common in all kinds of areas without ever laboring in jobs, naivety finds that working in migrant or minuscule jobs aren't significant anyway or are a benefit toward greater attributes. Only thinks that high tech and things that pertain to particular criteria will help improve themselves. Fortunately, according to the testimony of past and present successes, the greatest skills and learning of lessons in which to improve and become greater in all aspects of physiology comes from observing and learning from the common citizens' ways of functioning in all walks of life and ages, from infants to the elderly. Therefore, whether an individual wants to make money and advance in physical attributes or obtain greater knowledge, the best and most effective way is to observe and understand common people's daily struggles. And all the antics or mechanics that the individual must study in which to further themselves are just technical pieces of puzzles that'll come into play as each progressive training intensifies.

While working toward particular skills may take a lot of time in the daily schedule, to be rare and exceptional amongst all others, the individual must go the extra mile and do the unthinkable. To be something beyond human imagination and vision and obtain greater measures in performance, the individual must go and do where others would not. And while money will always be the greatest obstacle, the best training and lessons to be learned usually come from the most dreaded and unwanted jobs. This is why there are individuals who may have touched or felt the abilities of superior form but never got there, because in their hard efforts and dedication toward a craft, they only trained in flat and superficial methods, where they only thought and worked within modern ideas of conditioning and training in jobs and lifestyle.

The very first pioneers in achievements, whether mental, physical, or spiritual, were the rawest form of explorers and inventors, and in successes they stood out amongst the rest because their ideas and original blueprints existed for a long period of time, which modern enterprises try to duplicate but never come close to fulfilling, even though they've trained and worked just as hard. Though modernization made daily struggles simpler and less difficult compared to ancestors, in turn the old ways of training and discipline slowly dissipated, which made future candidates weaker in determination and willpower in achieving goals. Through modernization, the human physiology has weakened in defense and offensive attacks toward ambitions and goals. In turn, through advancement of logic in assessments, humans lack innovative thinking and visual stimulation in the impossible being achieved. In the old days, where modern comforts and economic opportunities were fewer, any individual who had aims to be something better had to walk many more miles in travel distance, determination, and persistence. And because they didn't have the financial resources, they had to obtain low-paying jobs while at the same time still training to fulfill ideal ambitions. And while training tactics and techniques were helpful in shaping and improving original conditions, the simple hard work amongst common'laborers' surroundings gave them the greatest perspective in understanding themselves and the many ways in which to approach a dream.

It's undoubtedly hard, perhaps nearly impossible, to break the old stigmas of achievements, and if any modern individuals are going to improve the old ways, they will have to pass through predecessors' ways of training and discipline, because as the human race advanced into the twenty-first century, they were foreordained to propel themselves into the futuristic world of superhuman beings, where overpopulation and continuous economic shifts will create chaos and confusion. In turn, the caretakers or future recipients must be ready and mentally susceptible to handle more intensifying crises in adaptability to overcome their worst weaknesses and deformities in which to become greatly admired and inspirations to teach and guide future generations toward greater sensibility.

These few expressive words may be heartwarming and morally inspiring, but the intended message is not for all superior beings to be righteous and become particular in purpose of being some kind of protector or savior. Rather, when entering a new millennium, it's inevitable that the human race will reach new heights in its ability to withstand degrees of suppression. Therefore, the few sentences of inspiring words of good omens, duties, and obligations were not intended as being the means and purpose of an individual improving and creating a better self. Rather, within the automated instincts of humanitarian virtues in being an intellectual species in ever-changing advancement toward greater prospects of future existence, most will try to obtain superior abilities for the good of mankind and helping the weak. Unfortunately, in the universe, there must and will be certain individuals who will use the power of superiority for greed and selfish gratification by abusing the accessibility within a structured society. Nevertheless, in whatever way an individual sees their existence and the role they must play within the social order, the ongoing conflicts of prejudice and contradictions in means and purpose will continue as long as there's signs of civilization.

After choosing a place of shelter, either privately or in a group, having extensive security will not be in best interest, because constant moving and job changes are a necessity. The next thing is to find some kind of occupation, and whether it's high-paying or distinguished is really irrelevant. Although, the more money an individual makes, the less the daily struggles. In waiting and wanting to escape the monotony of uncertainty and to find some other avenue in which to focus the attention, it's better to occupy time with things of learning, even in prejudiced institutions like various charitable or delinquent facilities. In those predicaments, it's all up to the individual's perspective, societal availability, and economic status, so it may take some time depending on location and personal criteria. Nevertheless, whether self-sufficient or financially supported by others, for the sake of wanting to find other possible skills for improvement and well-being, the best choice is probably the one that will allow obtaining independence and widening horizons.

Those becoming superior beings are rare; not many with comfortable lives or who are notoriety seekers will go deeper and want more complications with the pressure of expectations. Therefore, after whatever hours of energy are put into a particular skill, it's highly unlikely the individual will want to spend more toward a tedious, slow, money-making job. Instead, they would rather spend time on social affiliations or personal hobbies to take their mind and attention away from training and emotional loneliness. In turn, rather than continuously maintaining a train of thought, they'll break it with some mental distraction. The days should be kept busy with some kind of work to keep the body in good physical condition. If the individual has imperfections and the inferiority complex that comes along with poor physical appearance, then they will have better reasons in maintaining strong discipline.

Although mental strain and fatigue is understood to be present, and the individual wants to break from the monotonous and constant suppressive lifestyle with some enjoyment, unfortunately that's the big difference between limited achievers or those who make it for the long term. While short-lived superior acts are trained with breaks and interference, to be the best and exceptional, the idea of a break, vacation time, and hobbies are something that does not mix with the intensity of trying to evolve. The mental train of thought will continuously change, like a roller coaster. In turn, every time the mind is distracted by something pleasurable, the individual will have to start over again in the race to obtain the high level of mental focus necessary to accelerate the energy of power. That is why the individual must have an extreme level of discomfort within genetic makeup to being socially inept. Otherwise, they will not have level of desire necessary and will easily get distracted by wanting to have fun.

Although they may feel relief and rejuvenation from relaxing, it's nothing more than an illusion of the conditioned mind, and what they feel in the alteration of mental fatigue with the distraction has slowly lessened the acceleration of the energy of mental focus. In turn, when the individual has escaped their training in maintaining train of thought, they have slowly and steadily decreased the heightened point of acceleration, and when they return to training, they must start over and readjust their conditioning to focus. Therefore, rather than starting from their already accelerated position, they are starting from some low point from the lost time or financial limitations. While they could have obtained a higher and more intensified level of energy of focus, because of breaks and distractions from training, they will be emotionally compromised and confused about the future. Nevertheless, no matter how many times an individual tries to escape or detach from the intended goal, there's always the possibility of still fulfilling the mission; it's just a matter of the individual needing to internally renew the desire to succeed. Although taking breaks or quitting the course of training may not be great, fortunately life and its endeavors has no definite direction or conclusive way of accomplishing them, because there is always the possibility of redeeming from whatever failure or obstacle as long as there's an unrelenting craving for the chase.

The mind is in constant expansion within its progression by many things, including temperature changes. Although the eye cannot see or measure the energy changes either positive or negative, but it is influenced by various things like external experiences, the intake of elements, to different chemical alterations that are triggered by influential physical things like taste buds, emotional characteristics, and temperature. Hence, the internal working of the human mind is constantly eradicated, which prevents extreme energy progression that separates normal-level function from higher intellectuals, because their daily functions and lifestyle routines are different. Even the simplest daily rituals, like brushing teeth, showering, or even eating particular foods, can have a great effect on energy limitation and intensity. Therefore, every time an individual changes the chemical balance within physiology, which is the core of daily functions, it will take a rare individual with advanced mental capabilities in which to control and obtain the steadiness of mind that increases the energy of ability and performance. Because of the automated conditions that separate humans from the wild primates, humans are constantly changing their chemical balances in eradicating inconsistency.

Rather than having a mindset that has the stillness of water and steadily increases in acceleration, like the primitive's simple life energy of aggression in hunting and long times of passive relaxing, human life is all about commotions, tastes, and alterations, and they will forever continue to be deprived and prevented from obtaining higher levels of thinking to becoming something extreme. Hence, when an individual is trying to become something of greater proportion and obtain superiority in skills, they must let go of the feverish humanistic things and become almost primitive in aggression and obsession, in turn changing and controlling their lifestyle and automated way of thinking.

Whenever an individual tries to climb the mountain of achievement, it's not the mountain or physical mechanics that will create conflicts or complications toward the intend goal. Rather, because they've adapted to the humanistic way of living where they must constantly produce and disperse daily energy into various avenues in maintenance and personal hobbies, when trying to take on certain tasks in specialized form, they must produce extreme levels of energy while at the same time continuously dispersing it toward living a life full of family and friends. Because the individual doesn't know any better and lacks experience in the price and consequences of becoming a greater being, during the journey and climb they will experience chaos and confusion with new obstacles and complications. While an individual who has no distractions of family, friends, or hobbies, with the only obstacle producing the willpower for the exertion of energy, for the normally nourished with plenty of emotional support and certain lifestyle tastes, the climb to achieve will be a lot harder, almost impossible, compared to one who knows isolation and has adapted to loneliness as if it were a common thing. Because humans try to obtain abilities of superiority while still wanting to live humanistic lives, an individual has complicated their existence and pursuit more than what it needs to be. If they had no distractions from social affiliations, materialistic things, holidays, birthdays, or anything else that hampers, the task would not be as nearly impossible as it is, as long as they had the willpower.

Strong disciplines in physicality, refueling, and adaptability are vital elements in living an immaterial as opposed to a comfortable one. If an individual eliminated all social affiliations and the love of things like hobbies, they would have the highest potential in becoming a future successor compared to others who disperse daily energy into crafting personal tastes and associations, becoming a superior being and obtaining expertise like that of a genius or a godly figure demands a lot of sacrifice. All humans seek and continuously reminiscence on individuals who have become greater and left a mark, but to become one, or even something like them, is unfathomable.

Unfortunately, all the great achievers and mythological figures with record breaking accomplishments in every aspects of physiology are still a long way away from being the representation of a superior being. Although humans have categorized and made great systematical achievements, they are merely based and compared with society's standpoint of what is considered acclaimed. Therefore, although there will always be the famous who are recognized as having succeeded in doing something great, unfortunately they are just a glimpse of the potential that the human species can achieve. As long as individuals continue to live in conditions where they are comfortable and supported by family and friends, they are merely superficial replicas of what a true superior being can be. Although they may be accredited for their accomplishments, they are infantile achievers compared to what can be conquered.

Throughout history, the average human being has only used a certain percentage of mental capacity, nowhere near the maximum overdrive the mind possesses. Therefore, whatever successes humans have recognized, they are merely mortal beings whose lifestyles, affiliations, and interests have created vulnerabilities toward wanting to expand into greater heights, because to become truly exceptional, they must not let anything of human affiliations have any affect toward that mission. Most importantly, to become a superior being, an individual must not fear losing anything, from emotional attachments to material things or even death, and let themselves become exempt from being deterred from their goal. Moreover, they must embrace isolation and loneliness, where the fortress of solitude provides the greatest avenue in which to obtain the power of sensitivity that is the true giver of special abilities.

Whether an individual has found a job or not, the journey to become greater should progressively proceed through daily rituals, and crafting skills should slowly change for the sake of bettering themselves. The biggest obstacle, and greatest challenge, is finding the distinct pathway, and that will happen at an unpredictable time within routine schedule and depth of experiences. Nevertheless, an individual must live and train as best as they can with all the necessary mechanics that will contribute to the intended goal, such as physical conditioning and improved work ethics.

In the meantime, as time progresses from days to months to years, they must learn to reserve and eliminate unnecessary energy burners by changing certain rituals in their lives. For example, a lot of material things like clothing and furnishings should be cut to a minimum so that doing things like laundry and cleaning are easier. Also, each room should be vacant of any digital gadgetry or even unnecessary decorations, because during a mission to become greater, staying home becomes the least of concerns. Reading material can be permitted for collective information, but not purposely or abundantly, because relaxing in leisure or sitting around and waiting for opportunities will not be in their best interest. Other distracting things likes cellphones, excess amounts of accessories in a wallet, or dangling objects on keychains should also be eliminated, because these moments are not for extravagance or socialization; they are to obtain the highest level of energy, focus, and intensity. The need for security in locking the house and having stress over personal materials will not be important because of living in obscurity. And although having a bed may be acceptable, for ease in the case of needing to be mobile, such as unpredictable situations happening quickly, the fewer things a person has to carry and move will be most beneficial, not only for cost-effective reasons, but in wanting and needing to move efficiently, having less will always lessen the complications. Basically, an individual only needs a single room with a few items of clothing, and since they are in training, they should be alone and not be distracted by anyone, like female companions or even friends.

This mission to be greater and obtain certain superior abilities will ask nothing short of maximum determination in mental and physical discipline. Anything that is a possible distraction and will interfere with the daily ritual of training to maintain strong focus must be sacrificed for an indefinite time. If an individual just wanted to obtain another building block of superficial success, then just few years of working can easily get them in a better life position, because through a strong work ethic and discipline, they can get promoted and progress into prosperity, but to be superior in depth and diversity, they must wait for more promising dispositions.

Nevertheless as each month passed with solitude and constant training, an individual's mental energy will continuously increase in depth of understanding and purpose. The ideas and thought processing that once seemed hard will easily come into play in understanding the geometrics of a particular field of trade and its characteristics. This will be the crucial moment of finding out about an individual's existence and potential. In those moments, what was once thought as important or relevant will become clearer as to how far they wish to take themselves in reach for superior abilities, such as will the individual be satisfied with a certain degree of success or want to learn more in which to become the most extreme. If the individual trains, maintains their focus on the intended goal, and does all the disciplined research in how to succeed, instead of sitting around or wasting time on unrelated things, the individual will succeed and have some kind of resolve in a shorter time, especially if they truly followed a suppressed and meticulous way of life.

Unfortunately, if an individual succeeds and finds themselves with some kind of compensation in rewards, either by nature's good fortune or their doing, this will create limitation. In life, humans seek fast results and profits in whatever effort and time that they've invested on a particular project, and although it's easy to be tempted and coerced into accepting the potential of hard work, they have only touched the surface of the real training that needs to be done. Although an individual thinks themselves to be something of a great achiever, compared to future potential, they've only achieved a limited amount of success. Through a lengthy suppressive lifestyle, if they have succeeded in their mission to be, they've tainted themselves in becoming just another categorical achievers of accomplishments, and within success, they will be more susceptible to becoming another common figure amongst the masses. Even though they may have earned some kind of recognition and financial gain through early success, they will slowly fall back into the mold of society.

Although humans seek to achieve in earliest attempts, if they fail and are shunned by society and develop some kind of mental disorder, then they are on the right path in which to obtain the godly powers and knowledge in which to become superhuman. The problem lies in how long they can hang on and climb out from the dark and soulless dungeon of mental torture, and at what moment will they recognize the journey at hand that could make or break their well-being and get lost within the dark world of the unattainable.

Humans have always heard and been mystified by the ancient Asian philosophy of how energy pertains toward enlightenment and obtaining a greater sense of power. Even within scientific reasoning and understanding, the geometrics of how energy can be harnessed in which to produce maximum effect has the same fundamental idea—such as, if energy is generated and condensed into a specific form, it will have most potential or influence—but if all the energy is dispersed, the potency or strength will be lessened as it's spread into other outlets. Therefore, when it comes to acceleration and power in effectiveness, both spiritual and scientific ideologies give the same analysis in how to obtain maximum benefit in collection to storage and then in a particular moment of release.

The human body is like a big battery, and within daily functions and intricacies, they produce and exert energy toward an array of things. If individuals are involved in higher, concentrated activities, then more energy must be produced, but they must recuperate and rest more frequently than others who are not. While humans have shown uncanny abilities in all parts of physiology, with the human need to restore their energy, they are unfortunately inexperienced about knowing the limited degree of intensity in exertion as well as potential power. And although they may have achieved great feats with greater skills, because of living and associating periodically in comfortable, social lifestyle, there were limitations. When it comes to producing the energy of a superior being, they must have a more intense level of mental focus and discipline within life. They must learn to be more meticulous and mindful in the usage and conserving of power. Therefore, besides giving up personal hobbies and social associations, they will have to control certain attributes that are automated necessities of being a dignified species, likes taking showers, changing clothes, or even personal hygiene and grooming, anything that creates unnecessary irritations.

The frequency of energy in mind shifts from changes in hormonal balance through the five senses of touch, taste, feel, sight, and smell. The energy of mind is in constant motion, like an algorithm graph in up-and-down motion. It's rare for the mind to stay still, where the energy motion is in minimal to unwavering steadiness like calm water. For the mind's energy to accelerate, there must be reserve storage for that particular purpose. This is why a lot of artists, especially in moviemaking, fans often see their supposed perfect actors on screen look totally different in real life, extreme body disproportions, because artists produce energy from one extreme to another, from being active to lazy. Some are known to use alcohol and cigarettes in both enduring the monotonous waiting period for next project and staying lean, which commonly has health ramifications. This happens to all areas of professionals who have to deal with extremes. Nevertheless during that period, the mind is sedated and unenthusiastic about anything. Hence, the vibrancy of life and enjoyment has descended so far that it may cause mental psychosis to the point of depression.

At the same time, within the willingness to continue living by going through the minimal amount of daily motion, depending on the surrounding activity, the mind continuously collects information on the person's creative interests and endeavors. Although the individual is living life of a zombie, the mind will subconsciously collect all sorts of data which will either be beneficial or useless when they arise from their unpredictable state with constant conflicting mental turmoil of whether to continue on the intended mission or change direction toward the inevitable outcome. Although this stage of development seems that death has won and the end is near, fortunately, in order to obtain the hidden secrets of the unknown in deeper thought processing, the mind must travel deep into the subconscious in continuous acceleration in the negative aspects of collective energy, just as a black hole absorbs and distorts planets to produce hydrogen for the particular purpose of recharging Earth and the outer universe. Therefore, while every component of their physiology seems to be in comatose, within just a glimpse of light and hope somewhere deep within, the mind, body, and spirit that have been awaiting for a trigger or motive in which to resurrect itself from depth of unfathomable has finally come in terms of fulfilling the intended fate of destiny.

There are two different particles of energy that are responsible and a great influencer on learning lessons and obtaining knowledge toward greater heights, and while both have their own definition in negative and positive effects, such as being logical and enthusiastic, the individual will go about intended goals with full force, not knowing the consequences of possible failure or rejection and either being too logical or neglectful in taking chances of opportunities. And while some will slam into a wall of rebuke and be susceptible to giving up and heading toward self-destruction, there are others who are more ignorant and have primitive arrogance, where they had been rejected so many times but still pursue fantastical dreams. In their attempt to retain persistence, they learned and obtained the valuable lessons in which to further growth in maturity and intellect. Therefore, while there's inevitable cost and negatives in learning the lesson, and in the moment it seems futile or irrelevant, in their determination and finding some kind of resolve to carry on, when they have arisen from the depths of impossible odds, they'll reclaim their rightful rewards or compensation in what nature owes in either a blessing or a curse. Through the depravity of falling into darkness, they have gained and learned more lessons about becoming something greater than they could have ever imagined.

Although life and the choice to chase after greater sensibility and the unimagined may have consequential effects even for the most positive and optimistic people, as well as have costly repercussions of being slammed and denied that would lead toward many casualties, through some glimpse of inner desire to fulfill the internal instinct to be and followed, there will be a light even within the darkest times as an example of a most impossible situation to be conquered. Whether the individual has climbed up or down the mountain, humans have overcome and accomplished the impossible, but the price and consequences that were paid can never be witnessed by anyone other than themselves. Nevertheless, as humans revolutionize and overpopulate, there will be more candidates who will try the impossible feats of superior beings, and whether they achieve or fail, they will never be compromised as being folly or wise in their decision to attempt the mystical imagery of being something beyond.

In daily existence, humans have an automated way of dispersing energy, and while cultures differ in the amount of things involved in daily survival and maintenance, within ever-developing social conditions, all cultures will eventually have to adapt to modern sophistication, even most primitive cultural worlds in distant islands and jungles. Therefore, while the earliest human disbursements of energy were simplified in refueling and sheltering, while revolutionizing themselves to be a greater species of beings, they have metamorphosized their original form into something more complex. But in reaching for the maximum source of energy, the individuals must change society's automated way of living to maintaining certain regimens by cutting out unnecessary things. For example, when managing clothing and cleaning them, an individual doesn't need to fold or keep clothes in perfect form and put them in a specified place. Rather, find a large box and put everything from undergarments to casual wear into without wasting energy in ironing or folding. In turn, every time they need to change, they don't have to stress in producing energy on irrelevant things like the impatience of temperament, having a hard time managing things because they are too distracted by personal affairs or being undisciplined. It would give a pathway for the simplest and efficient motion without needed annoyance.

Because humans have been conditioned in the proper mannerisms for survival and maintaining themselves, they disperse most of daily energy into cleanliness and different associative hobbies. While certain things can be eliminated, such as social affiliations and personal hobbies, all humans must maintain certain attributes with physical attire, and the complexity of it lies in dependency. But in becoming something superior or obtain higher skill, the individual must learn to adapt and make use of better and more perfected ways of managing things that may be unorthodox but less of hassle mentally. Therefore, when it comes to clothing, they must and should keep everything in the simplest form, where they are producing and exerting the least amount of focus. So, find any kind of disposable, cost-effective container and just throw the clothes into it, but for professional use, such as a meeting or special occasions, the individual should keep a few outfits that can easily fit into one duffle bag to keeping them tidy. In this period of training, the individual should not have a need to impress or try to attract anyone except within professional situations like an interview or promotion. Therefore, how they look and the management of their residence is irrelevant, as long as it doesn't collect unwanted bacteria growth.

The other main needs, like eating utensils and kitchen supplies, should also be kept to a minimum, where limited time is spent on cooking and cleaning. Rather than having countless eating utensils and containers, they should just be a few like minimalists or prisoners. Often, humans collect things they never use and have too many unnecessary things. The individual is only one person and, especially in the situation of training and focusing, there will be no one else, so in trying to keep things clean, having more than the needed accessories only becomes a burden. Therefore more cups and silverware are unnecessary and will only collect dust and occupy space. Even in the moments when there is the need to sit down and eat, platforms like milk crates, wooden stools, or empty boxes can be used and disposed of easily, rather than investing in a table and chairs. By keeping everything simple, not only will the individual save energy, but the focus and motion will be a continuous flow, with more energy toward work or personal interests. Hence, they won't have to deal with shifting in a different direction or being irritated by obstacles. Although it may look barbaric and desolate, as if they were homeless or in prison, but the ability to focus and concentrate on the intended goals, conserving energy, and keeping mental stability will be nothing short of a necessity.

Through modernization and evolutional change, the human mind has lessened in focus and training in rawness of simple form. In turn, their mind has been twisted and turned every which way in confusion, especially with sudden career changes and economic shifts. Therefore, in the expansion of wanting to excel and obtain steadiness in focus, like the earliest hunters, through modernization and advancement and an easier lifestyle, with things like various gadgetry and material things, humans have lost the simple way of thinking and working, burdening themselves with heavier loads of unnecessary things, in an attempt to conquer and excel in specified fields. While most will attempt to become greater, they are ignorant of understanding the necessary sacrifices that are required. Instead, they will try to climb the mountain with heavier than necessary loads.

The other vital things that must be given some attention and that are considered to be frequently producing energy, like personal hygiene in brushing teeth and wearing particular footwear or cologne, should be done more precisely, by the simplest of means in choosing the most effective use or even eliminating it. Although maintaining personal hygiene, smelling good, and even having a distinguished hairstyle is important, but as long as the individual isn't associating with anyone, keeping themselves smelling good and having an immaculate physical appearance is unnecessary, unless for meeting an acquaintance or a professional reasons. But keeping the teeth clean and preventing them from decaying should be done, but the method will have to be very precise. If the individual is not constantly eating or drinking various beverages that easily stain the teeth and brushes them thoroughly, not haphazardly but with precision, the teeth can go for a couple of days without brushing, especially when living in an environment with good oxidation, like fresh air or working to stay fit. And such things as managing the hairstyle should also be kept in simplest form, where the hair can stay in one form without having to comb it for days, because every time energy is used for tedious things like the fixing hair, showering, driving vehicles, putting lotion on the skin, or any other maintenance toward appearance, the more mental focus and flow of energy will be expended. Hence, using minimal effort for physical attire and appearance for few days at a time will be most beneficial.

Through history, there have been many extreme energy producers, both famed and irrelevant, who have neglected the most basic maintenance, which caused their teeth to rot and required dentures. This may be accepted within common people, but when movie stars who have given the imprint of the most beautiful and perfected genetics that many fans admired and dreamt of as a possible love partner, then it becomes a shocking revelation. It is caused by extreme energy production toward personal ambitions but neglect in daily regimens. Nevertheless, certain things, such as teeth, must be maintained periodically, but with a good and complete cleansing, they can do without assistance for certain amount of time. And since the individual is in training, the smell of good breath is not a priority, especially since constantly eating and drinking sugary drinks will be nonexistent.

In these times, being alone in isolation while training should be the main concern. This may sound very bizarre and uncharacteristic of a dignified living being, but with the need to concentrate and focus most of the energy into constant acceleration, the lesser energy spent toward the smallest, unnecessary things, the greater surge of power and more reserves the individual will have, not to mention less mental irritation that will keep away stress and headaches.

The other important factor that humans must rely on and constantly maintain is refueling themselves with some kind of food. While eating may be an essential element in survival, there's a fine line as to how much and what kind of food is needed. There's an overwhelming problem with physical shape in society, and while there may be everything from extreme obesity to malnutrition in the young and elderly, even without the physical overture of disfigurement in size and shape, most humans eat more calories than they need, even if they aren't overweight. When training, the type of food needed to remain healthy is very important, with the digestive system rarely having bowel moments because the nutrients are all natural and being dissolved by high-impact physical exertion. Nevertheless, while some kind of training in the journey to be superhuman may require a greater intake of nutrients, like various athletes, for the majority of mental trainers in artistic creativity and those seeking greater mental capability seekers, the amount and type of food is really not a main agenda for daily existence. They wish to eat good food, but in their mission to be and become, eating substances and the amount of time invested in it should be irrelevant and not a major concern. Instead, they should eat and be able to adapt to whatever is available or affordable, but it should be real food, not processed, because their limited amount of food intake must be nutritional. Therefore, although food is important, within the mission to accomplish and become, eating should be the least concern.

Nevertheless, within the daily financial pressure, especially living independently and being self-sufficient, the individual must have pre-planned agenda on how they will provide the food and cook. Because while in dream world food just seems to be prepared to be eaten, when living alone and having to be concerned about the amount of energy that's dispersed and wasted toward preparing it, the individual in training must look elsewhere or calculate how they will continuously feed themselves without burning unnecessary energy. And while eating fast food and various snacks may solve the problem in saving time and energy, besides the unhealthy factor and the amount of money it will cost them in the long run, without vital nutrients, not only will the individual run into financial problems but their mental and physical state will eventually not perform as efficiently, no matter how healthy they may perceive to be. Therefore, in reaching for greater mental power in focus and capability, the individual must find a way in which to make most cost-effective, fast, and ready meals. Every individual would like to eat healthy and have the best conditioned body. Unfortunately, based on financial resources, the amount of time invested toward their craft, and also mental and physical fatigue, the individual will succumb to becoming dependent on commercial foods rather than buying cheap organic foods and prepare them as if it were gourmet cuisines.

Every individual was conditioned and learned life lessons in different ways and styles. Hence, if they were pampered and had easy access to every daily needs, then they are more prone to rely heavily on financial resources in which to fulfill nutrient needs. But the individuals that were raised in a suppressive life, where one grain of rice was valued as important, and they have learned to turn wasted products into something useful, then even in most financially strapped situations they are able to survive and eat richly, depending on cooking skills. Nevertheless, every living thing needs to eat something in order to survive, but when individuals are training to improve physical attributes, dietary consumption should be in best of nutrients available in a cost-effective manner. Depending on what part of the physiology the individual is aiming to perfect, the amount of food and type of nutrients should be recognized, but the amount is unnecessary.

Although they may have a cost-effective way to secure food and necessities, they will have other financial burdens, which is important for learning lessons toward knowledge and future endeavor. Nevertheless, whether its purpose is refueling the system, hygiene, clothing, or maintaining living quarters, the individual must learn to reserve their energy and store it for the upcoming tasks of crafting a particular specialized skill. In turn, they must try to spend less time on humanistic things like trying to look perfect or having items that will overcrowd their life and not contribute or have any relevance toward intended goals.

When it comes to personal welfare and well-being, it'll be very cold and isolated, and if an individual comes from the flowery world of love and decorative surroundings, the odds of them succeeding in their attempt to be some superhuman are nothing short of impossible. That is why the comic imagery of Superman, the strongest of all other superior beings, is always foretold in a fortress of solitude, because while every superhero deserves the rightful claim to be, no one is as powerful and indestructible as the infamous, heroic Superman.

There are other ways in which to increase the intensity of performance, but as long as an individual lives with things beneficial toward the mission to be and not on feverish, distracting things, within their daily time expenditure, they are forced and will eventually generate energy into things other than humanistic gadgetry and associations. There may be better and more intense ways to increase mental power, such as sleeping on the floor, which will have a greater amount of oxidation and restoring of energy in recuperation than sleeping on a bed. While any decisions of limiting and enduring a certain lifestyle may be within an individual's perspective. on the basis of wanting to do things more effectively and faster, living in simply with less luggage to carry when having to move and being forced into a world of deprivation is better. In an unexpected situation such as being left out in the cold because of losing employment or living quarters, the future seems uncertain as to where they will sleep and how they will ever continue the mission. Therefore, having more gadgets and furnishings is not really needed; in a time of moving, they will only create a great burden in travel and finances. Even simple things like chairs and a mattress can be an unnecessary burden and inconvenience.

In becoming and improving themselves in whatever they want to achieve, everything must be kept in its most minimalist form, even using disposable things. Being superior means the individual is able to do things faster and more effectively than commoners. Therefore, everything from personal antics in management to physical survival should be kept in simplest form, where there aren't any hassles or irritating decisions to be made. Even something as simple as wearing various kinds of footwear or jewelry should be eliminated unless it pertains toward a particular purpose. Although a common or non-high-energy producing individual may not notice the irritation of back-and-forth movements, in time, depending on the level of intensity, those minor things will have a great effect in the production of energy in performance and mental irritation. Therefore, in the phase of training, the best choice is if an individual eliminates and doesn't do things that are tedious, like locking doors, carrying small humanistic items, or tending to superficial needs. This might sound too farfetched and bizarre to absorb and endure. Unfortunately, to maximize oneself in the potential energy to be obtained in skill or performance, especially in becoming something beyond human capabilities or achieving something greater than already standardized or commercially made superhuman feats and imprints, the individual must eliminate as much hazardous and non-essential things as possible. Hence, they are left with a lot of time within a daily schedule in which to work toward particular interests.

The mental and focus energy must be in continuous motion, and the less it goes back and forth dealing with humanistic activities, the better equipped the individual will be for training.

The main thing is to make everything from outerwear to housing to interests be as minimal as possible. Also, the size of the living space should be limited so an individual can come and go quickly, without having to worry or be distracted by keys, phones, wallets, and other things. Therefore, having a dining room or any other extra space in the interior is unnecessary. In fact, extra space to clean and move around will only make them unnecessarily waste energy, making it a more complex way of living. And as far as maintenance and keeping clean, the room is bare of things, so cleaning will be simple or unneeded. But for the sake of staying free of bacteria and sanitation reasons, no food particles of any kind should be present. Because when living in filth and not cleaning, it's the edible substances that will create hazardous situations, endangering with diseases and bacteria, but there's no harm from dust collection, unless it's a biological ailment.

Through elimination and neglect toward common society's way of dispersing energy, the individual can conserve and only use it for a main agenda. In turn, more time spent toward a particular skill should give them greater ability to progress. By eliminating social and conventional ways of living and maintaining, the individual has the greatest potential in which to enrich their mental power of energy toward greater heights. That is why certain individuals who are considered geniuses or have very high mental skills have some kind of quirk, a nerdy personality or physical appearance, even unsanitary homesteads. While they may be exceptional in specific areas, in the everyday, common world they are considered weirdoes or freak of nature, because they invested all their time and energy into one spectrum and neglected things of social conduct. Although they may represent as a greater specimen amongst the populous, even with accomplished feats and superior skills they are far from truly obtaining and possessing superhuman abilities, mostly through aging and humanistic-conditioned striving for mental energy and being born in the time-consuming development process in education, where their visions and barrier breaking were long fought and struggled against society's ways, especially taking breaks in the prosperity of lifestyle, and in between trying to achieve superior ability, it has taken them decades.

Nevertheless, it's not about how fast and what age an individual accomplishes. Rather, within their own time of need and nature's intent, they will become and arise from depravity to prevail. Unfortunately, with nothing more than the internal call of natural order to be stronger and better equipped to overcome obstacles and show superiority, humans have automated themselves to be in some kind of competition in which to prove self-worth. In turn, the human race has fated and preordained their future to be nothing more than a continual and never-ending cycle of challenges to see who is the best.

There's twenty-four hours in a day, and while a certain percent are spent toward sleeping, the rest of time is within personal discretion. Since the individual is on a mission to become something better and more improved than what nature has given, they should spend as much time into crafting of skill. It's really not hard to excel in a certain trade of particularity, even though common people may find it difficult to near impossible. Although naivety may think that the genetically gifted or the ones showing the earliest potential may be the best candidates, but its more within the unexpected, inferior, and socially inept. Nevertheless, any individual that seeks to become something greater can condition themselves toward superior form, but they must endure an indefinite time of dedication and break away from a conditioned lifestyle of comfort. Even for individuals who don't have a specific agenda or plan on what thing they want to advance but want to obtain a higher sense of individuality in future prosperity, they can live suppressive and listen to inner self in what they could become.

In this lifestyle, the individual has positioned themselves to eliminate all commotion and distractions so that they can concentrate and focus within distinct placement. Although the lifestyle may seem harsh and inhumane, in wanting to do more and become a greater being, there must be sacrifice and struggles. Therefore, within the isolation and solitude, away from time-wasting, irrelevant, and mindless things that common people invest their one and only existence into, the individual has the opportunity to listen to an inner voice calling out particular fate and destiny. They could even set extreme financial goals to be reached so there is some reason for entering the suppressive lifestyle until nature takes its course.

Humans are always, and forever will be, chasing time in which to prolong life. Hence, they always say life is too short because of having lived within automated society full of abstract and materialistic things. In this deep meditative time of finding oneself and living a life totally absent of superficial and time-consuming things, the individual has the power to do something about it. And whether they are in pursuit of a particular skill or are listening for a special calling, they all will have to challenge themselves to obtain the best collection of energy and transform into something they could have never fathomed. First is living very simply, without any gadgetry or unnecessary furnishings, like monks or other people who shun material things. The second is to find some kind of job, not so much for financial reasons, but because working and independence always builds character, ethics, principles, and discipline.

In becoming something beyond the conventional, an individual most definitely will have to work and learn the struggles of common people to earn rightful place in the unorthodox realm of the accomplished. While this may seem argumentative in perspective or irrelevant because doing it alone and leaving family and friends is too hard and should not matter, Mother Nature's intent is if an individual was destined to become, nature would take its course by intervening in a time of need. Hence, the individual will succumb or adapt to nature's accordance by putting them in situations with conflicts. In turn, they will have to choose to either give up or die trying.

Human physiology has three major components that will become their greatest attributes or adversaries in excelling into superiority. Only two are tangible, where they may have the power to control production or destruction. The soul can only be felt by an individual's enthusiasm and desire, unlike the mind, where they have the choice to observe and learn. With the body, the individual has the power and control over what kind of physical activity to do in training, how long, and what the dietary requirements are. In accomplishing superior feats, it's a very rare individual who has excelled in the combination components of physiology. Such as, if an individual has become an intellectual extremist likes various academics and artists, they usually neglect the physical, athletic attributes, and any of the extreme physical achievers usually neglect intellectual creativity. The reason is simply because as they try to craft a distinctly specialized skill, they have invested whatever time they had into that particular field while at the same time living a human-conditioned life with gadgetry and social associations. In their attempt to become something of superior form, they also wanted to live and have personal interests toward things like taking breaks and vacationing. Because of this, humans, in an attempt to achieve whatever extreme ability, not only find it hard, most do not accomplish their goal and slowly enter suppressive conditions in an array of mental deformities. Even if they did obtain some success, they often fall from supposed notoriety whilst imprinting themselves to be exceptional.

Unfortunately, no matter what area of physiology improvement that has been accomplished for notoriety and recognition, the amount of mental power, physical exertion, and surge of power that was used is small in comparison with what could have been put forth. Therefore, whatever area an individual wants to craft or perfect, it's better if they have a better balance between mind and body. Because the soul is invisible and pertains to spirituality and particular beliefs, the increase or decrease in the amount of energy will come from their will to succeed and not wanting to fail.

As far as what kind of mechanics an individual should use to enhance a particular field is within their understanding of the geometric and metaphysics of the skill. For example, if an individual is looking for the mental and thought processing abilities either in spiritual or calculative things, then it's nothing more than researching present and past world-renowned intellectuals and being observant. It's better if they endure chaotic and insecure experiences that could have life-threatening effects rather than studying materials, but the journey of expanding and evolving themselves toward future prosperity will never end. And while the naive would like to succeed with a few years of effort, unfortunately, to become exceptional and obtain superior abilities in whatever degree, the learning of lessons with continual trials and tribulations are necessary experiences that must be experienced. This will separate the ones that were destined to be with the ones who just want a quick and easy pathway to superiority. Nevertheless, while most will stop and just accept their limited conditions and become another building block of society, those with the strongest convictions and belief toward the intended mission will continue, ignorant of limitations, while others who fail will just become another distant memory.

When it comes to anything from physical skills to intellectual abilities, an individual must continuously try to work better and more efficiently than others, no matter how tedious the task, because when trying to break through the barrier of the unknown and obtain knowledge and superior skills, it usually comes from those with the strongest discipline. In the meantime, they should keep their body strong by doing the required exercises to stay in top condition. As there are many with the potential to accomplish superior feats, so are there many possible ways in which they should train and discipline themselves to become both mentally and physically fit. Therefore, the particular things that should be done and the best way of doing them will all depend on experience and the amount of dedication put towards it. But one thing is for sure, the greater and more intense the training toward reaching for glory is, the more power and higher level of energy and oxidation by the simplest of living conditions endured. Moreover, they have put themselves in the position of having more open ground by eliminating unnecessary things, where they will have more time and energy in which to heighten skills. If they were to follow a strict and rigid way of life by being totally independent and persistently striving to be for long periods without breaks or vacations, they will easily have a greater depth of training and discipline that will make previous contenders become irrelevant in comparison.

Unfortunately, it's easier said than done, because as each year passes without any warmth from humanistic things and associations, an individual will become more susceptible to delusions and getting lost in thoughts that could easily lead toward a depressive abyss. Therefore, as each progressing season gets colder for both flesh and soul, not knowing where to find for warmth and the uncertainty in the continuous stagnation of life for the foreseeable future, and within the constant agony of maintaining limits of jobs and dedication toward an ambition that is nowhere in sight, the individual will be left with two possible alternatives: either come back to the land of common people and live the tedious lifestyle of emotional embodiments, or eliminate themselves from the competitive world.

Thirdly, the individual must try to neglect as much of the tedious back-and-forth energy burners as possible, such as changing clothes, organizing a home's interior, or even grooming and dressing themselves so as to impress. It has to be done periodically, but it should be done when it's really necessary, like every couple of days, because every time an individual moves or alters movement, where it may cause a change of temperature and perspiration, it will interfere within internal energy flow. Even simple things like getting wet or eating tasty foods, especially spicy or tangy ones, the frequency of energy changes. Hence, it's very rare for the mind to obtain steadiness, except when sleeping. Things like driving vehicles, where the mind must be constantly alert and shifting energy back and forth, are the most distractive to mental focus. Hence, when in training, driving should be eliminated. Instead, use the old-fashioned way of traveling, like using public transportation, biking, or simply using your legs.

The sensitivity of mental faculties will not be recognized until decades later in situations like self-defeat and confusion in life's direction, so its paramount that a person's physicality is naturally strong and not corrupted by excess nourishment. In the mission to be the best and more profoundly tune themselves in specialized skills, an individual's mind must be in a constant state of processing and finding solutions for particular obstacles and agendas. Hence, whether riding on the bus, walking, in the toilet, or simply sitting to take a breath, their mind is constantly in tune with the objective.

When living independently, the most crucial problem will be lack of financial resources. Depending on an individual credentials in the job world, the amount of money made to fulfill daily necessities will vary. Even simple things as a toothbrush or toilet paper could be a burden, perhaps not in the first few years, but most definitely as the time of training stretches into decades. In reaching to become something illogical or fantastical in wanting to be rare and superiorly conditioned, they must have the ability to be frugal and creativity. Hence, the true candidate will not be academically acclaimed. Rather, they'll have irrelevant work credentials and be unimportant, likes immigrants or a school dropout who feels the unrelenting guilt of failure. In turn, the individual will be left with limited availability in job choices and have minimal income.

In fulfilling daily necessities they will have to be resourceful, eliminating even more unnecessary materialistic things. Also, having enough money or credit in which to lease or rent a place to live will be highly unlikely. At times, they will have to use society's charitable resources like shelters or religious organizations in which to survive the most difficult days in suppressive life. If the individual has too much pride or is pessimistic toward religion, that could be a determining factor in survival. It will all depend on their acceptance of misfortune and not to shortchange themselves by rejecting the helping hands of others.

Being alone and living independently with its burdens and mental agonies is something that cannot be explained in words. Hence, minor problems like washing clothes, having to cook, or deciding what to wear will cause more stress and complications than they've experienced or expected. Therefore, while maintaining themselves as a dignified being in necessary, the individual will have to rely on physical capabilities, like in the old days, in which to do the laborious work of maintaining in the simplest way. At first the individual will start by making certain concessions, depending on preconceived hang-ups or conservative way of living, but in reaching to become something of greater worth, there will be just as much turmoil in consequences as sacrifices to be made. So, while in the beginning individuals will have certain perks like excess dollars and being highly enthused about their new venture and lifestyle, as time progresses the initial feelings will slowly sway and change.

Humans are destined to change in both good and bad ways, and whether or not an individual succeeds in an attempted mission will not stop the evolutional change of human species. Therefore, as many aspire to be greater, only a certain few will come out of the darkness and proclaim their journey as a triumph. And whether they'll be recognized for achievements or forgotten, an individual has categorized another building block in possibilities that society will secretly talk as being either truth or fiction. In turn, others will try to follow in their footsteps, but the invisible lines can only be seen by the next contender worthy of carrying on the burden of revolutionizing the human race and creating new visions and ideas in which to give future generations the innovative mind to create their own fate and destiny.

There's no limit to how far and deep the human physiology can be manipulated in which to obtain surges of power in energy. And while they can control a certain degree of mechanisms in how they increase their mental capacity, either positive or negative, through vitality and enthusiasm in or a righteous lifestyle or a destructive one, Mother Nature has the ultimate control of how the human mind can sustain and influence the energy capacity by dispositions and unexpected situations to be experienced. Nevertheless by living and eliminating all things that may distract mental focus, like humanistic things and associations, and also living in certain suppressive ways, the individual has some degree of control, just like plugging in dead batteries to recharge them.

While limiting movement of tedious things and living in an open space may contribute to a higher intensity of mental focus and performance, there are other things that will give ultimate control to restoring energy, such as sleeping on an open bed or floor with a mattress in vacant space full of fresh air, or blindfolding your eyes when sleeping, with blinds that blocks out all light, to obtain the most potent effects of brain power. While the modern method of higher brain function usually pertains to meditation while sitting and focusing, taking short naps with blinders is a more-effective storage of energy. This fits into the scientific reasoning of how the mind and potential of energy is the most effective in storage. Hence, if the body and eyes are in motion and not in a relaxed state of laying down, then the level and potency of energy is compromised.

The hardest thing will be to adapt and control the hyped and conditioned energy from normality, where an individual that has high energy has problems sleeping or relaxing their body. Because society is full of vibrant of energy and full of spirit, it is sometimes difficult to relax outside of the time when the biological clock says it's bedtime. Hence, trying to sleep during the day will be the hardest thing any individual will have to attempt, especially for an uncertain period of time, like a long, sedated form of meditation. Nevertheless, just as all energy-powered things wear out and must be recharged in order to be functional, the human body has the same fundamental basis. The more it's rested, the greater potential ability it has in recovery toward a higher level of function in completing intended tasks.

At the beginning, the individual may be too preoccupied within daily actives and obligations, but eventually there will be a time when training must become more serious and intense. Although it may be easy to understand the practical thing of objects being recharged with some kind of instrument, when it comes to a living organism like human physiology, measuring and detecting the good or poor levels of energy is impossible. Hence, through both good and bad actions, there could be some ramifications, because as an individual obtains a higher level of mental energy and focus, they're susceptible to becoming irritable with others. Because while they may obtain a stronger sense of awareness and discipline, there will be opposite effect of impatience.

Many high-energy producers have been using this method that common people could never imagine, likes famed movie stars, athletes, and spiritualists. Unfortunately, there have been some who have entered into the meditative state of obtaining higher energy but somehow succumbed to giving into the darker side in destructive ways because they could not handle the constant insecurity of personal goals and lifestyle. They became an example of the possible repercussion of entering into the world of intense disciplines. Although it's never proven scientifically that how an individual acts determines the level of energy, on the basis that good and strong represents being in control of conscious thoughts, the negative has been overpowered by the subconscious controlling illogical acts of destruction. Hence, there is possible danger in obtaining a higher level of focus and energy because society lives and function mindlessly with irregularity and limited brain function. Therefore, although humans are forever seeking to obtain higher intelligence and capabilities, it could become more in negative of influence in daily functions and activities. Hence, only certain individuals could ever endure and overcome the journey of the unattainable.

No human seeks to do things that may destroy themselves or society when born, especially when every being started out as an infant without conscious thought of planning into the future. Nevertheless, somehow during their developing years certain individuals have obtained higher levels of energy that triggered or inspired them to do both productive and destructive things. And although positive or highly intelligent levels of mental capability is responsible for exceptional achievements and easily accepted and praised, when an individual has become lost and is out of control, acting out in beastly and inhumane ways because life or society had forsaken them, the intensity of energy have taken over the logical senses, and they are easily dismissed and never recognized as having potential to be a greater specimen. In whatever way humans improve and try to obtain extra powers, there will be those unaccountable who will succumbed to a surge of mental power and will do unimaginable acts, both positive and negative, just as in earliest days of creation. Even though the world and everything in it may be superficial and all that exists from beginning to end may only be an illusory perspective of how an individual sees and pertains life to be, within ambition and instructed world of motion and imagery, humans are and will always be in competition to be the best and most accomplished breed of Homo sapiens.

Superhuman

There are many means and interpretations in which humans define and categorize being superhuman. Although it is used more superficially in which to detail and give credence to individuals who could do amazing feats that society can't see themselves being able to do, the word is used very loosely or most profoundly, depending on ideology and perception. Through human history and finding ancient relics and documentation that were discovered by experts, there were certain pictographs, graffiti, and actual written evidence in foretelling human figures with unbelievable stature. And although modern artistic skills and illustrations have greatly changed in the depth and degree in which certain humans were shown as superhuman in dramatic imagery, through history there have been many human beings doing and representing something beyond the common, but to what degree their skills and capabilities led them to near immortality will remain an ongoing mystery still to be discovered. In the meantime, as the human species continuously evolves, there arises more superhuman imprints and capabilities that future generations look upon as inspirations to overcome their own deformities and imperfections. Nevertheless, while the idea and image of superhuman figures are often shown through physical abilities, what is commonly envisioned are limited to being extremely distorted by naivety. Hence, there is no depth in the true representation and contention of being superior.

Humans have always been fascinated by superhuman figures through childhood influence in comic books, and on dramatic and animated television programs. These triggering mechanisms have inspired many, from the innocent children to even the most sensible adults. Although logical thinkers could differentiate between reality and fiction, what many thought as of childlike entertainment and visions were and continue to be the greatest of ideals of how to achieve and overcome limitations. Hence, what was presumed to be something unrealistic and fictitious has given some the will to strive to reach their innermost sanctum of the unattainable. Most of it pertains to gimmicks and trickery for personal notoriety and commercial purposes in various kinds of physical performances, from the most intense professionals to childish things within mental, physical, and even spiritual faculties. Nevertheless through their will to be and show things that could be accomplished within the vulnerability and limits of the flesh, there are endless ways of how flesh-conditioned beings could become and accomplish the most illogical and impossible feats.

Through modernization, certain individuals have studied and taken old stories of unbelievable doctrines and transpired them into visual creations. Whether it was for personal acclaim or just wanting to show others the possibilities or an amazing period of human existence, the visual imagery and metamorphosis of imperfect beings has slowly inspired and evolved into unknown depths. Although the actual time of contention and becoming will be controversial in the evolution to mortal form, superhuman abilities are totally different from the illustrative personification, because human flesh has limitations, but it gave other possible avenues in which they could become closer to superiority.

Although humans could never obtain the actual physical ability to move objects with kinetic energy, or the superhuman powers to defy atmospheric gravity, there are other ways in which flesh beings could portray as superhuman and give visual inspiration to others who may need some guidance and hope in time of struggles and limited vision. Therefore, through modern visual imagery in books, radios, and most importantly television and movie screens, the human mind has seen and then pursued in which to obtain greatness. For example, in Asian martial artists' array of methods and styles of developing superior mental and physical abilities that enable the vulnerable flesh to become impenetrable, to being used as the most extreme weapon in hand-to-hand combat, likes kung fu experts and ninja warriors.

While the dedication in time to enduring immeasurable pain and sacrifices can never be understood unless the individual has experienced it, through visual imagery and effects in the story and tactical choreography by dedicated experts, it gives naive observers the idea of unbelievable things that can be conquered and achieved. In the Western world, it gives other aspects of superhuman abilities by storytelling about social conflicts between cowboys and Indians in fighting and individual rare skills. Indian superiority may be shown through a certain chief's ability in hunting with a simple makeshift bow and arrow or conquest in battles, whilst the white man's skill is shown through advanced firearms, where the speed, precision, and distance of killing a target is shown. Then there are other superhumans shown through use of particular metal weapons like swords and knives in disciplined ancient arts in all cultures, especially in conflicts and war, but any simple object, from hairpins to playing cards, can be used as weapons through training and discipline.

While there may be many kinds and examples of superhuman feats, there were few rare individuals who were above the rest and recognized as being something supreme. How they came to be and obtained their particular skills may be a mystery to observers, just as their missions and fated destiny, but without written accounts and showing it in on the superficial platform of flat screens, the human race could not have advanced and evolved toward a greater sensibility of beings. Hence, humans are forever fated to continually compete amongst themselves in which to improve and upgrade from original simple condition.

Unfortunately, no matter the degree and depth individuals are perceived to be and what superhuman abilities they obtained, there's no practical use for it within the reality of daily existence. For instance, a martial artist that has extreme capability cannot stop bullets, can never become beneficial in distant combats, and can easily be destroyed by sneak attacks with modern weapons. Hence, the time and energy that must be produced in which to achieve and maintain that condition could all be wasted. Even if they were able to use it in self-defense, the individual would have to endure possible persecution and the inconvenience of the legal system. The only real benefit can be within wars, but those only happens for certain periods, not extending for a lifetime. Therefore, all the superior skills and abilities may look amazing, but in the reality of common life, financial obligations, and family welfare, it's an endeavor for an individual who lives a life of solitude for whatever reason. However, they too will eventually have to face the vulnerability of being made of flesh, like the repercussions of aging to uncertain economic shifts. Hence, the individual will have to succumb to dealing with changes and superficial imprints. This applies to all superficial achievements and recognition, because common people don't have an excess amount of time to invest in personal interests that cannot help toward daily survival, especially if it's financially costly or if they have personal addictions, like various substances or even sexual preferences, where continuous sustainability of discipline would be compromised.

If an individual were able to capitalize on their particular ability, it would give some benefit, to whatever degree, like appearing in movies or working in security, which are indefinite and unpredictable in terms of prosperity. Other than that, humans have no need for such extreme skills, even in dramatic situations like social conflicts or various crimes to the extreme example of terrorism, because it does not happen frequently. Therefore, although seeing and imagining a superhuman being sounds great, the reality is that it takes too much time in selfishness and the unpredictability of livelihood, which no mortal has power or control over, because even basic necessities like breathing contaminated air can cause individual lives to become irrelevant and expendable.

There is a systematical order of importance within the human social ladder, such as the rich are looked upon as superior intellectually compared to the poor. While the value and richness of life will always be an open debate and controversial, with logical understanding and better benefits, the rich or financially established are calculatedly smarter and understand the ways of life more sensibly than people who just live life mindlessly and cause illogical commotions and arguments. Hence, when achieving or proclaiming to obtain superhuman skills and abilities, there also has to be a certain system of importance in value and benefit, likes individuals who have established great financial wealth can easily overstep anyone who is superior in physicality or ability. Because within the resource of social power and position, they can buy any supposed superhuman figures within their disposal, like being a puppet master or having godly powers.

While it may be great to achieve superior feats to whatever depth, all flesh beings need resources for survival and are emotionally unpredictable and are tempted toward the possibility of easier or more heightened lifestyles. Hence, all those with superhuman abilities will eventually succumb to cashing in on their particular attributes for wealth and recognition. Although the wealthy and successful are rarely looked at as something superhuman, few have the willpower or discipline in which to obtain it. Because just as those in society in whatever culture wish and seek financial success, while many attempt it, only a few amongst the countless ever achieve it.

While there may be many examples of individuals who could do superhuman feats, the logical and sensible focus their energy toward the realism of obtaining true benefits in producing the discipline of mind in which to make money. They could have invested a childhood fantasy into a particular interest of hobbies and unessential attributes; instead, they put their superhuman effort of energy toward financial possibilities, because wishing to become and obtain is a long distance away in the production of energy and discipline of mind. For instance, an individual has to produce just has much willpower in perseverance as adapting and conditioning themselves toward unbelievable pressure in unpredictability of other competitors. Even though they may not have the physicality or acrobatic expertise in self-defense, through financial disposition they have the power of buying and using any flesh being within a particular interest. Therefore, whether the individual accepts the inevitable corruptive conditions of the flesh in the real world of survival or has conviction toward a moral compass in beliefs and merits, there always will be the individual who capitalizes on their hard-earned training and discipline compared to those who have some support system. Both are wise and being a folly, not because of life choices or endeavors, but because all flesh beings are limited and must face the inevitable repercussions in death. No matter the degree and depth individuals presume themselves of being or obtaining superhuman feats, they will all have limits and expiration within nature's accordance.

While achieving superhuman feats may be admired, there are certain characteristic traits that differentiate the true superhuman amongst the many other superficial superior beings that observers or fans could never have imagined. For instance, no matter if the superhuman individuals were foretold within the realm of martial arts, Western gunslingers, or even the biggest financial tycoons, they all contain well-developed, unmanly things, like domestic skills, the tedious disciplined trades like craftsmen, or various kinds of building capabilities from using raw materials. This may sound illogical or bizarre within the imprint of being most supreme, but when understanding how individuals would obtain the particular of skill over the persistence of time, in silence, and the never-ending obstacles and challenges, then it would not be surprising that those with aggressive personalities also have passive ominous traits. Unfortunately, it was not their intention, it was rather through some fate or misfortunes that the individual had arisen and become.

Therefore, through early development in whatever guidance to hard-laboring disciplined tasks that modern children often hate and rebel against, a most innocent child can become very extreme in capabilities. They are imprinted and shown all kinds of fictional stories in books and movies. Although most observers would just bypass it without any thought, heroic figures are often shown traveling through some town and helping certain people by having profound, unexpected skills, such as a lonely cowboy who can build an impossible sculpture or building that the townspeople's most experienced craftsmen could never have imagined or done. Or they could cook faster or more efficiently than any female or commercial chef or managing domestic things, like Asian warriors are often portrayed doing in fantasy, heroic movies. There are many movies and examples of unbelievable skills with superhuman figures that defy the logical mind, because within their image of the most extreme, in both productive and destructive characters, there contains the element of the simplest, like common people, but they could do it more efficiently and quickly, without tiredness.

While in the wild the females are the most aggressive in hunting for nourishment, it seems the human configuring of the superhuman has the same fate and feats in understanding, though it's questionable whether fans and admirers will ever understand these paradoxes and accept that their mother's domestic traits will be the greatest avenue for the discipline in which to become and achieve super-heroism. Nevertheless, through history to the ever-growing new breed of greater beings, the traits of disciplinary skill and focus continue to lie within the domestic skills or the tedious and monotonous trades that superficial superior beings might find irrelevant toward particular endeavor. This is why there is the popular saying that every man's success lies within every woman. Hence, every male or female's greatest accomplishment and success came from the strength and backbone of the supposed weaker sex, from the spouse to mothers and grandmothers. Therefore, whether human specimens have succeeded and become superior figures within physicality, the mental calculations of an entrepreneur, or obtained a greater sense within the spiritual realm, it all came from the blood, sweat and tears from their most prominent nurturer and giver of life.

Conclusion

In existence, everything from Earth to the outer limits of universe is fixed in displacement of order, which makes all things work together in a synchronized form. Through the force of energy that gives balance and organization in purpose and importance there lies infinite possibilities, and all things are predestined to happen within its time of necessity. While humans presume to be in control within social structure and construction of development, it seems they are merely going through the motions in what is already engraved and printed in cells, chromosomes, and invisible particles of matter. And through internal instructive and distinct purpose, humans have created a vast civilization with endless potential that has been specifically designed within nature's accord just as complex as the planets of the solar system.

Nevertheless, even though humans are powerless to shift and rearrange everything in the outer limits of space, within the inner sanctum of the earthly realm in nature and disposition of lives, they've shown the power to change the natural order to their own ideals.

Humans have the automated instinct and natural behavior of wanting something that is not common or envisioned within the superficial world. Through the production of hormonal vitality in characteristic of intrigue and curiosity, their appetite of need and desire are constantly evolving to new heights. They are destined to explore and seek new avenues to reinvent themselves into a stronger and more perfected species. The earliest human visions were following ancestral and predecessor survival disposition in employment, but through modernization and the expansion of inventive ideas and creativity, humans have strived for something beyond society's fundamental things and have looked to achieve greater things. It creates metaphysical mystery of why only some seem to have desire and dedication in which to achieve superior feats, but through inspirational stories and imagery of the impossible being accomplished, there is an opportunity for anyone to achieve superhuman things. It's just matter of how determined they are and how they see themselves in retrospect within displacement.

Since the beginning of time, there have always been examples of superior beings, which are documented in relics that gave propensity and proof of existence. Whether anyone truly believes the folk stories of historical events or not, as time revolutionizes the human race, there seems to be a continuous and steady growth of who can do the unimaginable. They have been fated to live lives of abnormality and become the next imprint and representation of exceptional. The reasons and what triggers them to aim to achieve may only be answered by themselves, but the sacrifice, dedication, and painstaking struggles that were put forth can never be appreciated in understanding difficulties. Therefore, although many may feel the inclination of wanting to be, only a few will go forth and overcome the impossible.

There is an array in which the human species has shown uncanny ability in superhuman feats, in significance to irrelevance. Although all superior achievements should be admired and appreciated, since it leads the lifestyle path away from normality in sacrifices of fundamental things in which daily time is spent away from social affiliations amongst friends or hobbies. Hence, the price might be too high with repercussions. They are separated and practically uninvolved in the things of the common people; their time is spent toward crafting superior skills. Therefore, while populous dedicates time toward loved ones and the abstract things in life, but superiors must obtain strong discipline and maintain focus by not getting involved in the festivities of relaxations, and not for a short time but indefinitely.

While achieving and accomplishing superior feats may be great in triumphs to conquering, but when having to live a suppressive or life of loneliness and sacrifices, like not having leisure time for simple pleasures such as sleeping in late or eating whatever the body craves, or simply accepting their distinct imperfect order of existence, it's hard to understand whether it's really worth the effort, especially on the basis that all things will eventually die. Whatever accomplishments, awards, or recognitions achieved will long be forgotten, only remembered by the naïveties who only reminisce and could never understand the strong convictions, determination, and moral virtues required. Therefore, sacrifice and suffering that were endured are reduced to meaninglessness. Nevertheless, as time continues to mold the human species toward never-ending ambitions and desires of constantly perfecting, there will be no shortage of superior candidates, but the intensity and diversity of challenges will be more demanding.

Everyone perceives and understands life differently, and whether achievements are recognized in notoriety or not, at a certain moment of life, all will feel some form of tranquility in being something beyond. And although there's a fine line between the truly rewarding feeling in superiority, like of famed and recognized compare to naivety moment of the pretentious euphoric rush in tediousness, whether greatly accomplished and symbolized or simply a brief passing of time, all are merely illusory perceptions of mental psychosis to lift and gratify in which to feel the potential power and exhilaration can be achieved. Therefore, while there may be endless accounts of superhuman who have trained and dedicated years to decades in sacrificing toward perfecting skills, there are others who have not selfishly put forth the energy of productivity upon themselves. Rather, they shared and distributed personal time into others who were in need of assistance in fighting struggles, and although they have never won awards or recognition in efforts to try to improve the world, if they had put forth the energy and time into training, they too would have achieved the impossible. Instead, in their fated life, they were destined to rescue and save the needy and helpless.

Then there are the parents and guardians of children, where they have invested decades of energy and dedication in guiding and teaching. Whether they succeeded or not should be irrelevant. Rather, the amount of time and energy that were exerted can be measured more than the necessity of achieving something superior. Instead, through selfless acts and dedication, they were willing to invest their time and energy into something more important and sacred than the personal gratification of rewards and recognition. It's understandable that training and conditioning to become more perfected is hard and demanding, but when countless who timelessly dedicate themselves to others without any pretense of expectations, it's hard to underline or define the motive that produces such determination, just as if they were training for a world competition.

There are all types of superior beings that have existed since the beginning of time but never been famed or recognized, and as the population and modernization grows and develops, there arises more avenues in which human species can perfect themselves and overcome the impossible. And although the true means and purpose of becoming and achieving the feats of a superior being may have different perspectives and ideals, they all have the same moral code of beliefs and constitution within the discipline of development, like serving and protecting the weak and fighting against negative forces that may cause destruction in all walks of life on the land, ocean, and sky. It could be simple as planting new seeds against massive deforestation to recycling while others neglect caring for the ecosystem. Some will continuously dedicate themselves toward the incurable social desolation of homelessness, while others work with the incorrigible addicts and criminals. Others will continue to invest in education and legislation, no matter the degree of modern corruption, pessimism, and disorder. There are endless examples, and whether they are spotlighted in recognition or just simply exists in the crevices of life amongst the rest without any metals or imprints in effort of helping, all superior beings are branded and have an unconditioned obligation to become an influencer and educator for future generations. While it's easy to recognize the commercially made successes, there are millions in all nations who are hidden from spotlights but continue to save and devote personal lives toward others who are in need or preserving the planet for a better future.

The idea of being superhuman may be flat in visual effects likes of movies and comics, but in the real world the characters and beings are conditioned in flesh and bone, where they feel the wear and tear of inner selves tiring because of everyday obligations, struggles, and limitations. Each day of motion that is produced, the flesh will feel the pain of tiredness in mental and physical fatigue, unlike the everlasting characters of the fantasy world. Nevertheless, there are some who feel they must do something to encourage the ill and unfortunates in which to give hope for a better outcome. Therefore, just as superheroes in superficial imagery are shown fighting against evil, through compassion and understanding of the helpless and the weak, they have designated themselves to take on the responsibility of improving the conditions of the bad into good, and because of this the world continues to exist. Most importantly, through excessive abuse of resources, things are savaged and prevented from early annihilation, had it not been for all the efforts that have dedicated their superior skill in humanity of heart.

Review Requested:

We'd like to know if you enjoyed the book. Please consider leaving a review on the platform from which you purchased the book.

CPSIA information can be obtained
at www.ICGtesting.com
Printed in the USA
LVHW040508021222
734355LV00005B/187

9 781682 357385